All the Presidents'
WITS

All the Presidents'
WITS

The Power of Presidential Humor

Gerald Gardner

BEECH TREE BOOKS
WILLIAM MORROW
New York

Library of Congress Cataloging-in-Publication Data

Gardner, Gerald C.
All the presidents' wits.

(Beech tree books)
Bibliography: p.
Includes index.
1. United States—Politics and government—
1945-   —Anecdotes, facetiae, satire, etc.
2. Presidents—United States—Anecdotes, facetiae,
satire, etc.   3. Political satire, American.   I. Title.
E839.5.G32   1986   973.92   86-8374
ISBN 0-688-05940-6

Printed in the United States of America

First Edition

1   2   3   4   5   6   7   8   9   10

BOOK DESIGN BY KATHRYN PARISE

The word "book" is said to derive from *boka*, or beech.
The beech tree has been the patron tree of writers since ancient times and represents the flowering of literature and knowledge.

To the Gardner Wits—
Harriet, Lindsay, and Joey

Contents

☆ Contents ☆

☆ *Contents* ☆

Introduction

"There are three things which are real—God,
human folly, and laughter. The first two are
beyond our comprehension, so we must do
what we can with the third."
JOHN F. KENNEDY

Political humor is no laughing matter.

All of our presidents from Kennedy to Reagan have had about them a cluster of writers to provide them with a steady stream of anecdotes and one-liners to project them as warm, witty, and wonderful.

Humor is a form of voter seduction that is more insidious than dirty tricks and much more amusing. It has been exercised with consummate skill by most recent presidents, but by none more effectively than the Great Communicator—who might more appropriately be called the Great Entertainer. Ronald Reagan demonstrated the considerable power of humor in winning to his banner a huge army of Americans, many of whom disapprove of his policies but who respond better to one-liners than to serious dialogue.

It should be recalled that in a televised debate with Walter Mondale, Ronald Reagan swept away the only obstacle in his path to a landslide with one inspired joke on the issue of age. On that occasion it became apparent to public figures of all parties and persuasions that political humor is a powerful weapon for winning votes and defusing issues.

The determined exploitation of humor by American presidents probably began with Jack Kennedy and has waxed and

11

waned through the past quarter century, depending on the character of the current White House resident.

Kennedy had a brittle, elegant wit that was augmented by that of his chief speechwriter, Ted Sorensen, and that he used to seduce the press, charm the public, and defuse such issues as wealth and religion.

Lyndon Johnson used humor to mask his fury at any criticism, and to present the public with a folksy, avuncular image while concealing his decidedly crude taste in comedy.

Richard Nixon's mindset was too bitter and insecure to permit the frequent employment of humor, but there were some sparkling exceptions to this vow of solemnity.

Gerald Ford was not a witty man—he seemed tone-deaf to the tempos of humor—and so he brought one of Hollywood's premier comedy writers into the august West Wing of the White House to brighten his soporific speeches with crackling one-liners.

Jimmy Carter found his way into the White House by presenting an image of rectitude and righteousness. He was suspicious of humor as alien to his nature and to the public need. Carter's sobriety got him into the White House, and it got him out again, when he ran into the wit and geniality of Ronald Reagan.

Reagan uses jokes more often and more adroitly than any president since Kennedy to advance his programs and to promote his views. Which raises the perplexing question: Why is it that if a man wishes to hold the most demanding position on the face of the earth, he must be able to tell a joke?

Perhaps it is because millions of American voters tend to vote for personality rather than policies—for cosmetics rather than character—for meaningless humor rather than meaningful programs.

Patrick Caddell, pollster extraordinaire, sees an ever-increasing emphasis in our political system on "style." We are developing, he says, a political system in which substance means very little. In such an atmosphere, humor becomes a very serious matter.

It is suggestive that the two most revered, most admired, most loved presidents of the past quarter century—Jack Kennedy and Ronald Reagan—were also the men with the most agreeable senses of humor. Kennedy and Reagan serve as parentheses to the Presidential Age of Humor, which not coincidentally also embraces the Age of Television—an era when charm and wit flow into every living room in the land, more accessible by far than wisdom or judgment.

It is an indisputable fact of American life that wit is a prime ingredient of political success.

The reason for this curious state of affairs is that under the American political system, we tend to nominate candidates to *win*, not to *rule*. And winning requires charm and wit rather than profundity and executive skill; charisma, not character.

As the importance of humor increased in the White House, presidents turned to the craftsmen of Hollywood, the traditional home of comedy and canned laughter. There has always been a symbiotic link between Hollywood and Washington, between entertainment and power. Robert Redford once played a senator; now several senators are playing Robert Redford.

Of course, the public has always been drawn to the theatrical in its leaders. Warren Harding was a splendid actor; unfortunately he was crooked to the core. Franklin Roosevelt was an extraordinary ham, with ghostwritten humor from playwright-speechwriter Robert E. Sherwood. Harry Truman's thespian skills improved with use until he produced a startling second-act curtain by defeating Tom Dewey. Ike had a movie star image complete with radiant smile. Kennedy was a superb actor and wit, a Potomac Barrymore. Lyndon Johnson was a superior raconteur and rustic humorist, though on the heels of Kennedy, the transition was like a dissolve from Noel Coward to *The Dukes of Hazzard*. Carter and Ford were wooden wits at best, supported by an assortment of comedy imagists in Washington and Hollywood. Ronald Reagan boasts an extraordinary charm and a genuine sense of humor, a major reason why the American public has responded to him with such affection.

In the American political process candidates and incumbents know that it is essential that they appear to be "good Joes." Nothing is more effective in creating this impression than a library of self-deprecating humor. No public figure should be without it, and none is.

Sad to say, many voters don't object to mediocrity in their president, but they absolutely insist on a sense of humor. Comedy writers can supply this humor in a dependable stream, and so our presidents are careful to keep their wits about them.

Our chief executive must please as many and offend as few as possible. And humor is one of the most reliable ways in which to please. Over the past twenty-five years, most of our presidents have realized that humor is worth its weight in power.

I came to know the potential of political humor in a very personal way. I wrote it.

When Bobby Kennedy declared his candidacy for the U.S. Senate from the state of New York, he invited me to travel with him as his resident wit. Bobby knew that I had helped create the popular satirical TV show *That Was the Week That Was.* He was familiar with my book of political satire *Who's in Charge Here?* He met me when his brother found a copy of the book baked inside his forty-fifth birthday cake and invited me to the White House. So when Bobby decided to make a run for the Senate, he invited me to board the bandwagon as his purveyor of relevant humor.

For the next ninety days I traveled up and down the state of New York with Bob Kennedy. It was my responsibility to provide him with humorous lines that were suited to locale and occasion.

I learned a primary goal of political humor: to defuse uncomfortable issues that will not respond to facts and figures.

The chief problem that bedeviled Bobby was the fact that the Kennedys were indelibly associated with the State of Massachusetts, and he was running for the Senate in New York. It seemed a flagrant case of carpetbagging.

"How can we dispose of this issue with humor?" Kennedy asked me one evening.

One line did the trick.

Kennedy opened each of his stump speeches with these words until the carpetbagger issue was laughed out of existence:

"People ask me," said Bobby, "why I came to New York. Well, a few months ago I read in the papers that California had passed New York in population. So I turned to my wife and I said, 'What can we do?' So we moved to New York and in just one day we increased the population by ten and a half." Bobby paused. "I challenge any other candidate to make that statement!" He concluded with mock solemnity, "My opponent has just sixty days to match that record."

I discovered another way in which humor can help a public figure—it can enable him to dodge an unanswerable question at a press conference, without resorting to a chilly "No comment."

When reporters were pressing Bobby to learn whether he was willing to be Lyndon Johnson's running mate, he was ready.

REPORTER: How do you feel about a Johnson-Kennedy ticket?

BOBBY: I'd be willing, but I'm not sure that Mr. Johnson would accept the Vice-Presidency.

Then there was the "ruthlessness" issue—the public image of Bobby Kennedy as the intense, relentless young man who had driven Jimmy Hoffa into prison.

In defusing the "ruthlessness" charge he said, "People say I am ruthless. I am *not* ruthless. And if I find the man who is calling me ruthless, I shall destroy him."

☆ INTRODUCTION ☆

In providing gaggery to Bobby Kennedy and observing his own spontaneous wit at work, I became keenly aware of the value of humor to a public figure in winning public affection and defusing dangerous issues.

On the pages that follow we will explore this strategy of seduction by laughter. We will see how our last six presidents have used wit and humor to have their way with us. It is not inappropriate to say that they have laughed all the way to the White House.

Part One
RONALD REAGAN

"I will not make age an issue in this campaign. I am not going to exploit, for political purposes, my opponent's youth and inexperience."
RONALD REAGAN

Chapter 1
The Age Issue

> "Reagan's people were convinced that the biggest problem he had to overcome was the perception that he was too old to be president. And so at every opportunity, Ronald Reagan did age jokes."
>
> BOB ORBEN

For Ronald Reagan, the troublesome issue of age never lent itself to logical discussion. It was an issue that was close to the consciousness of many Americans and hence could not be ignored, yet it did not accommodate reasoned debate.

It would have been unthinkable for Ronald Reagan to cite the latest research on how aging affects the mind. Ironically, those facts would have offered him substantial support. Most measurements show that mental ability is unaffected by age. But Reagan and his advisers could see the folly of a reasoned discourse. Facts would be unavailing in such an argument.

The only possible weapon against the age issue was humor.

Bob Orben, the dean of presidential humorists, recalled how Ronald Reagan and his hired guns had used strategic wit to keep the age issue at bay throughout his campaign against Jimmy Carter. Orben was well equipped to judge. In 1974 he had been summoned to the White House to enliven the speeches of President Gerald Ford and he knew the potency of political humor.

"Those age jokes," Orben told me, "essentially co-opted the

field. And Reagan's age got to be old news. If anyone wanted to question his age, they were done." Reagan had laughed the issue out of existence.

He used various jokes, all on the same theme and all in a similar form. He quoted Thomas Jefferson's comment that a person's chronological age should be no barrier to his service to his country. Then he would pause and say, "And when Tom told me that . . ."

Speaking to the Washington Press Club, Reagan mentioned its founding in 1919 and added, "It seems like only yesterday."

In a speech in Atlanta, he said, "I share with you the honor of this special occasion, the 105th annual meeting of the great American Bar Association." A presidential pause. "It isn't true that I attended the first meeting."

Reminded that if he was reelected in his quest for a second term, he would be leaving office at the age of seventy-six, Reagan said, "Well, Andrew Jackson left the White House at the age of seventy-five and he was still quite vigorous. I know because he told me."

At a Gridiron Club dinner, Reagan noted that the club had been founded in 1885 and told his hosts "how disappointed I was when you didn't invite me the first time."

Said Reagan at his seventieth birthday party, "It's just the thirty-first anniversary of my thirty-ninth birthday. I'm enjoying every one of them. And I think that it's fine when you consider the alternative." With this gibe, he managed to borrow simultaneously from Jack Benny and Maurice Chevalier.

Responding to Ted Kennedy's crack, when Averell Harriman turned ninety, that Harriman's age was only half as old as Ronald Reagan's ideas, Reagan said, "Well, you know, he's absolutely right. The U.S. Constitution is almost two hundred years old, and that's where I get my ideas."

Said Reagan to a group of doctors, "We've made so many advances in my lifetime. For example, I have lived ten years longer than my life expectancy when I was born—a source of annoyance to a great many people."

He returned to the familiar format of a chat with a Founding Father when he said,"I accept without question the words of George Washington, 'To be prepared for war is the most effectual means of preserving peace.' Now, in spite of some things you may have heard, he didn't tell me that personally. . . ."

And referring to Mikhail Gorbachev, who at fifty-four became the new Soviet premier, Reagan said,"It isn't true that I don't trust anyone under seventy."

Humor managed to keep the question of age suppressed throughout most of Reagan's first term. But humor had a useful ally in the restraint of journalists. Newsmen, in their self-acknowledged wisdom, tend to govern the rules of campaign debate. There are numerous matters, such as sex and senility, that journalists simply ignore. They exercise this restraint despite the succulence of these matters, or because of it. Their rationale for this self-censorship is the high-minded view that such matters are irrelevant to sober political debate.

This journalistic self-discipline placed tremendous pressure on the reporters covering Ronald Reagan, since by definition, newsmen report news, and from Hildy Johnson to Carl Bernstein reporters have not been renowned for their discretion. What punctured the bubble of restraint on the age story was Ronald Reagan's halting performance in the first televised debate with Walter Mondale. The President stumbled and stammered before a national audience. As satirist Mark Russell observed, "He's an actor and he acted his age." In truth, Reagan faltered no more than he had on those other infrequent occasions when his advisers had permitted him to speak without a well-rehearsed scenario. But in this case, the emperor was observed to be without clothes on national television, and Washington's newsmen felt themselves to be released from the bonds of tact. They reacted like dieters who have been told that chocolate is low in calories, or nuclear physicists who learn that fallout is good for you.

Throughout the campaign, White House reporters had

been kept a safe distance from the President. If there were signs of his advancing years, newsmen were too far away to observe them without the aid of a telescope. One newsman commented, borrowing a line from *Love Story*, "Covering Reagan is never having to say you've seen him."

Reagan's age may have been off-limits to reporters before the first debate made it a public issue, but it was open country to America's satirists. Said Mort Sahl when Chernenko ascended to power in the Soviet Union, "Chernenko is about the same age as Reagan. Between them they've seen Halley's Comet six times."

On the cover of the 1980 campaign edition of my quadrennial *Who's in Charge Here?*, I had a reporter saying to Ronald Reagan, "You said that you'd resign if ever your memory started to go," and Reagan replying, "When did I say that?"

The acerbic wits of *Punch*, Britain's venerable humor magazine, twitted the President's age and infirmities. It reported that he had acquired a hearing aid with a built-in digital clock. It told of a White House aide bursting into the Oval Office with the news, "Mr. President, Soviet troops are massing on the Yugoslav border! What should we do?" And Reagan replying, "About a quarter to six."

Candidate Mondale was careful never to question Reagan's age. A purveyor of humor for the candidate dispatched some light remarks that touched on the subject of Reagan's age, only to receive word from Mondale's campaign manager: "The candidate doesn't feel that's a fitting subject for levity." But reticence did not keep Mondale from accusing Reagan of "government by staff, policy by default, management by alibi, and leadership by amnesia." "Amnesia" was a code word for age, as were the implications of poor memory, failing eyesight, and reliance on others. All that was missing was the pungency of wit.

But the age issue was not an easy one for Mondale to exploit. Were he to have told a joke about Ronald Reagan's antiquity, he would certainly have been labeled a dirty fighter.

The canons of candidate etiquette are the reason why political dialogue in America is so boring, witless, and insubstantial. "What is American dry goods?" asks a character in *The Picture of Dorian Gray.* "American political speeches" is the reply.

Ironically, Mr. Mondale had reasons other than taste for avoiding the age issue. Democrats are supposed to defend the elderly from job discrimination. Federal law forbids ousting a public employee from his job because of his age. Reagan was certainly a public employee and Mondale had his eye on Reagan's public housing.

Between journalistic restraint, political etiquette, and his own arsenal of self-deprecating jokes, Reagan had little cause to worry about his chief vulnerability—until the age issue exploded on the scene after the first Reagan-Mondale debate.

Here was a good example of the limits of political humor. Though one-liners and anecdotes can seduce us into laying aside a particular issue, humor is a flimsy reed on which to rest a defense. When your own eyes supply the evidence, the seduced may regain their virginity. As Mondale said to Reagan in the second debate, "It's like Groucho Marx used to say—are you going to believe me or your own eyes?" The public was seeing Reagan's confusion and hesitation with its own eyes. More than any other president in decades, Ronald Reagan enjoys the adulation of most Americans, but as gagwriter Pat McCormick said, "The public is very fickle, as I was just saying to my cab driver Jerry Ford . . ."

After the press lost its reticence, *The New Republic*'s astute columnist TRB observed that perhaps we should treat our presidents as we do our college students and give them pop quizzes to see what they actually know. He supplied some sample questions for Reagan, such as "Who is the president of Honduras?" and "Name your grandchildren."

It might be said that he who lives by the quip shall die by it. Of course, Ronald Reagan had not expired after that first debate, but he was wounded. And the jackals of humor circled the body. Said Art Buchwald, "The President's advisers know that if he goes to sleep for even five minutes during the second debate, he'll be in trouble."

Four years of jokes—those countless conversations with Andrew Jackson and Tom Jefferson—were suddenly forgotten in the image of a tentative, incoherent president. Reagan approached the second debate with the caution of a man defusing a bomb, which indeed was just what he was doing. He need not have worried. Ronald Reagan had a large bank balance of goodwill with the American public. All it took was a fair performance in the debate and one inspired joke to satisfy the electorate. In attacking the President, Mondale was drawing a check on a bank in which he had no account. The people *wanted* to believe that Reagan was in great shape and up to the job. The famous joke turned the trick. . . .

The second debate was proceeding in a serious manner, with Reagan and Mondale exchanging simplistic insults on a wide range of subjects. Art Buchwald was observing that the President hadn't dropped off to sleep for even a moment.

Then suddenly destiny and humor struck. Veteran reporter Henry Trewhitt asked the President a predictable question. It floated up to the plate like a rookie's knuckleball.

> Mr. President [said Trewhitt] . . . you already are the oldest President in history, and some of your staff say you were tired after your most recent encounter with Mr. Mondale. I recall that President Kennedy had to go for days on end with very little sleep during the Cuban missile crisis. Is there any doubt in your mind that you would be able to function in such circumstances?

Translation of this painfully polite query: Are you too old to be president? Reagan positioned his feet in the batter's box and smiled slyly. Said Reagan:

> I want you to know that I will not make age an issue in this campaign. I am not going to exploit, for political purposes, my opponent's youth and inexperience.

Game, set, and match to Mr. Reagan.

In the wink of an eye and the crunch of a punchline, the debate was won and the election were over. As Jack Germond and Jules Witcover recalled in their vivid election chronicle *Wake Us When It's Over,* "The studio audience broke into sustained laughter which turned into enthusiastic applause." If the answer did not really respond to the question and was gloriously irrelevant to the issue, no one seemed to notice. Even Mr. Mondale seeemed aware, in a flash of prescience that his four years of electoral exertions had gone down the tube. He smiled the hopeless smile of the condemned.

Reagan had closed the door on Mondale's one glimmering hope with his most reliable weapon—the dreaded one-liner. Observers recalled how Ronald Reagan had disposed of Jimmy Carter four years before in their televised debate. Reagan had used a single pungent one-liner to destroy the Georgian. "There you go again," he had said in equally irrelevant rebuttal to Carter's attacks.

Ronald Reagan's line about Mondale's "youth and inexperience" was caustic yet funny; it produced waves of laughter in living rooms around the nation, and the waves washed away Fritz Mondale's final chance.

Foreign observers said that there is something frivolous about a political process in which a candidate's sole chance for a comeback could be demolished by a joke. Humor may decide other matters of importance in a democracy, such as the choice of Best Original Comedy Screenplay, but it should not have the power to choose the American President.

Chapter 2
The President's Wit

"It's amazing how important humor is considered to be in this town. The power it has—what it can do *for* you and what it can do *against* you."

LANDON PARVIN

Landon Parvin was Ronald Reagan's premier comedy writer during his first term in the Oval Office. But like so many other White House aides from that period, Parvin has moved out into the private sector. With Don Penny, former comedy adviser at the Ford White House, Landon Parvin now serves a bevy of political luminaries in the consulting firm they share in Georgetown.

Parvin knows better than most just how effective is the Reagan wit and how powerful a tool it is in maintaining Reagan's huge constituency. Looking ahead to the humorous demands that leadership will place on some of his famous clients should they reach the ultimate position of power, Parvin told me, "Ronald Reagan has changed the landscape when it comes to humor. Because post-Reagan it's going to be expected. I don't think people realize how he has changed what is going to be expected of a politician."

Then, with a knowing smile at Don Penny, Parvin added, "It's going to be good for speech and comedy writers like Donald and me."

* * *

Landon Parvin reached the pinnacle of chief comedy writer to the President by a circuitous route. In getting his graduate degree in labor relations he found he could get better grades by putting humor in his term papers. "Teachers were so bored from reading term papers," he said, "that when they found some humor they'd give you a good grade."

In San Francisco, Parvin joined a group of comedy writers who worked at punching up businessmen's speeches, for modest compensation.

"So I decided to go to Washington to do it," said Parvin.

He wrote comedy for Mark Russell, who proved a useful conduit for the young writer. Russell put him in touch with Rich Little, for whom Parvin wrote political humor, and the editor of a Capitol Hill newspaper for which he wrote a humor column.

Since Washington is a town in which the value of humor is widely acknowledged, Parvin found that businessmen were calling on him to enliven their speeches with comedy. Then, a local public relations firm, Hill and Knowlton, hired him to be its Washington speechwriter.

"The head of the office," recalled Parvin, "was a fellow named Bob Gray who was a friend of the Reagans and co-chairman of the 1980 campaign. He recommended me to the White House." The rest is history—and comedy.

Parvin was in an enviable position on the White House staff. Most speechwriters wince as they see their work wend its way through the White House bureaucracy, revised and altered all along the way. Not so with Reagan's star comedy writer.

"Since I was the only one who knew about humor there," said Parvin, "no one ever touched what I wrote. It just went in to the President.

"The White House is not a place that understands humor, so if you were a person who *did* understand it, they left you alone to do what you did.

"Technically the humor went through the head speechwriter, but fortunately he understood that humor is in the eye of the beholder, so he never did anything to it. He didn't know what the President would pick out."

Parvin was grateful for the discretion exercised by his superiors. "You really can't have people editing humor," he said. "If everyone on the White House staff who was in a position of power took out one joke, you'd end up with nothing."

If the chief speechwriter could not anticipate which jokes Ronald Reagan would like, neither could Landon Parvin. He would generally submit from three to five pages of jokes to the President for a given event so that Mr. Reagan could exercise a choice. And Parvin was often astonished at the President's selections.

"Some of the ones I thought were the best jokes he wouldn't use, and some that I thought were weaker, he would take."

Parvin mentioned one of the chief perils of writing humor for politicians—the influence of the wife. Making it perfectly clear that he was not referring to Mrs. Reagan ("She never got involved"), Parvin described the Spouse Problem.

"You can have what you think is an exquisite script, and the fellow likes it, and then what invariably happens is that he goes home and reads it to his wife. And his wife will say, 'Oh, *that's* not funny!' The spouse is deadly to humor because she thinks she knows what's best for her husband. So I try to keep it away from the wives."

Parvin is constantly impressed at the importance that Washington politicians attach to humor.

"I got a call the other day from a well-known Democrat whose name I won't mention. I went down to his office. He's now out of government and in private business. And his secretary told me, 'He's got millions of dollars of business hanging and what's he worried about? A funny speech that's not till next year!' "

Many of Landon Parvin's clients are still very much in government. Indeed, his client list embraces virtually all the GOP presidential hopefuls for 1988. He instructs them all in the employment of humor, and how to deliver a speech with the style and aplomb of Ronald Reagan.

Whatever their political coloration, Parvin's clients share an admiration for the rhetorical and comedic gifts of the President—his impeccable timing, his relevant humor, his modest demeanor, his optimistic tone. They know that Reagan's speaking style—with an important assist from the wit of Landon Parvin—has been a vital ingredient of his immense popularity.

When Ronald Reagan speaks, his performance is formidable, a thing to be envied and emulated—from the husky voice to the twinkly eyes.

If these mannerisms and that upbeat wit can be grafted onto a Baker or a Dole or a Laxalt, Landon Parvin will be propagating a remarkable strain of Reagan clones to strike fear into the Democratic party.

Chapter 3
The Disengagement Issue

"We'd end up with the President telling funny
stories, anything from old anecdotes about
Hollywood characters to something that happened on the ranch."
ARAM BAKSHIAN

The problem of portraying Ronald Reagan as totally in
charge has bedeviled his White House imagists for a long
time. Ironically, it is Reagan's sense of humor that has com-
pounded the trouble. His taste for rambling anecdotes has
often given him the appearance of a man who is not on top of
his job.

Reagan would turn a meeting with top advisers into an occasion for humorous anecdotes about his days at Warner
Brothers.

A visit from a foreign dignitary in which the leader made
an impassioned plea for arms control concluded with Reagan
exclaiming, "Say, have you heard the one about Brezhnev
and the Warsaw hotel?"

A meeting with congressional leaders on some urgent legislative business would turn into a monologue on the fun-filled
days at the Screen Actors Guild.

Reagan's nostalgic wit was contributing to the feeling that
he dropped in and out of his job, like a cameo star on *The Love*

Boat. This quality concerned his advisers, who stopped maintaining the fiction that he worked very hard at his job.

Indeed, they tried to make a virtue of his lassitude by drawing odious comparisons to Jimmy Carter, whose compulsive work habits seemed to produce little besides frustration and failure.

The question of whether Ronald Reagan is actually on top of things has always been a sensitive one at the White House. It sprang to life when his aides failed to wake him after American planes engaged in a dogfight with Libyan jets. Then Reagan slept through part of a meeting with the pope, and adviser Michael Deaver admitted that Reagan had slept through parts of several Cabinet meetings.

Said a White House humorist, "There are only two reasons you wake up Ronald Reagan—World War III, and if 'Hellcats of the Navy' is on the Late Show."

One congressman was appalled at how often he had gone to the Oval Office for a talk on some crucial problem and spent twenty minutes listening to the President tell funny stories about his sportscasting days with the Chicago Cubs.

Aram Bakshian was Reagan's chief speechwriter during his first term and would sometimes grow impatient with the President's propensity for substituting anecdote for policy.

"Once a week," Bakshian later recalled, "we would have a meeting where I would take some of the speechwriters who were working on whatever the main projects were that were coming up—and some senior staff—and we'd meet with the President. And generally it was scheduled for fifteen or thirty minutes, but generally it ran over. . . . We'd end up with the President telling funny stories, anything from old anecdotes about Hollywood characters to something that happened on the ranch. . . .

"The meetings," sighed Bakshian, "were for the purpose of planning some of his speeches, but they just turned into neighbors chatting in the backyard. It's just the way he is.

31

"You'd see Jim Baker or Mike Deaver looking nervously at their watches," said Bakshian. "On more than one occasion I had to end the meeting. I had to say, 'I know you've got a lot of other things to do, Mr. President.' If I didn't, we'd still be there."

Inside Washington, Reagan is the butt of humor that disparages his intellectual gifts. Ted Sorensen tells a joke about Reagan asking his barber to place a black dot on his forehead. The barber hesitates but Reagan insists.

"But Mr. President," says the barber, "a dot on the forehead is a decoration in *India.*"

"I need it," says Reagan. "I just met with the Indian ambassador, and after a few minutes of conversation he turned to his aide, tapped his forehead, and said, 'Nothing there.' "

Ted Kennedy recently mocked Ronald Reagan's disengagement from his own government. He said, "People may be sharply divided over the Reagan administration's policies—but they should admire Ronald Reagan for not getting involved in them."

What some see as disengagement in the Reagan personality is actually the heart of his appeal—it is a humor and a serenity that is immensely attractive to the public.

Said *Time's* Hugh Sidey, "Reagan is not that serious about himself or his views. He promotes them but he doesn't worry them. It doesn't worry him that people don't accept them universally, or that journalists oppose him, or that commentators scoff at him."

Reagan seems to be able to laugh at his critics and at the whole absurdity of the human predicament. His humor is part of his personality and flows from a deep sense of security. One feels that when crisis strikes, it doesn't ruin his day or sour his stomach. He turns it aside with laughter. "Say, do you know what Bogart said to Cagney in the Warner commissary?"

* * *

If there is any justice to the observation that Ronald Reagan is not very scrupulous or attentive to the details of governing, that same passivity is not observable in his attitude toward his speeches, and particularly the humor that enlivens them.

Aram Bakshian recalled, "I used to spend a lot of time writing funny lines in the President's speeches. Then I'd see them taken out by the President in favor of better lines that he would add."

A familiar refrain among comedy writers for U.S. presidents and presidential candidates is that the jokes they inserted in their patrons' speeches were killed as being either insufficiently funny or relevant. Those bitter complaints were expressed by the comedy writers of Jimmy Carter, Lyndon Johnson, and Gerald Ford, to name but three. But rarely is the presidential taskmaster adequately gifted or concerned to replace the anemic joke with something better out of his own repertoire or creative imagination.

But according to his West Wing humorists, Ronald Reagan is not a man whose ego and pride of authorship impedes his ability to appreciate the wit of others. He warmly welcomes funny one-liners or felicitous anecdotes that will draw a laugh and make a point.

"He's very easy to satisfy," said one White House wit. "He's extremely easy to write for."

This contrasts dramatically with the attitude of Jimmy Carter, who was suspicious of humor from his in-house wits and responded best to jokes, however tasteless, that arrived in the Hollywood pouch.

Reagan contrasts even more markedly with Lyndon Johnson, who felt that humor was beneath the dignity of his august office and would pass along to Vice-President Hubert Humphrey any jokes that he felt were unworthy of the presidential seal.

Reagan knows the immense value of an appropriate and laconic one-liner. When the Congress threatened to send him a budget-busting tax bill, White House writer Josh Gilder fed the President a crack appropriated from Clint Eastwood's Dirty Harry movies.

"Make my day," said Reagan.

The line brought laughter on the four, five, six, seven, and eleven o'clock news. It long outlasted the occasion of its use, which is the mark of a successful presidential quip.

Like John F. Kennedy, Ronald Reagan is probably his own best comedy writer. It is a matter of time. But Reagan finds the time to retool his speeches and spends more hours revising and rehearsing his speeches than any of his predecessors in the Oval Office.

Critics of Ronald Reagan—and they are surprisingly rare for a man who has made such profound changes in our society—suggest that he spends altogether too much time polishing his prose and not enough time attacking the problems that beset the White House.

Where does the Reagan time go if not to studying the complex alternatives of presidential action? Well, a good deal of the time he is rehearsing witty monologues for delivery to the numerous press dinners that dot the calendar in Washington.

These journalistic banquets, at which Washington newsmen proclaim their own self-importance, are so numerous that Reagan's in-house writers and his Hollywood contributors are kept busy supplying the President with a steady flow of one-liners for these joyous affairs.

Most presidents have attended at least one of these dinners, often as a reluctant duty. Some have ignored them entirely.

Said Landon Parvin, with evident pride, "Reagan has attended every one of them! Except, of course, the year he was shot. I don't know of any other president who has done that. Presidents are usually afraid of them and go to maybe one during their term, but they aren't at ease doing humor."

This presidential reserve is not surprising. Standing before a vast group of people and trying to make them laugh can be a daunting experience. But not for Ronald Reagan.

"President Reagan really enjoys these press affairs," said Parvin. "So he not only goes to the Gridiron, he goes to the White House Correspondents Dinners, he goes to the Alfalfa Club, he goes to this one and that one. . . ."

Comedically speaking, Ronald Reagan will be a tough act to follow. "After he leaves office," said Landon Parvin, "I think other presidents are going to have hard shoes to fill. They won't be able to do as many humorous dinners as he does."

John F. Kennedy was a voracious reader of history. He tore headlong through books on government, world trends, and the lives of statesmen. He wrote two bestsellers and won a Pulitzer Prize. If Ronald Reagan has read anything beyond movie scripts, say his critics, the fact is unrecorded. The books in his library were chosen by a decorator and remain carefully dusted.

How does Ronald Reagan deal with the disturbing question of his intellectual credentials? As with the question of age, he laughs it right off the record.

He often kids his mental laxity and thus makes his listeners feel it is not worth their attention.

Visiting a grammar school classroom, Reagan told the students:

> I thought maybe you asked me here to a remedial English class because you heard my speeches.

Returning to his alma mater, Eureka College, to deliver the commencement address, Reagan mocked his academic achievement at the institution. Said the President:

> I only came back here to clean out my gym locker. . . . But I am excited to receive this honorary degree, since I had always figured that the first one was honorary.

Reagan could manage to laugh away his modest scholastic achievements:

> I confess I was not always attentive as I might have been during my classroom days. I seem to remember my parents being told, "Young Ron is trying . . . very trying."

Said Landon Parvin, "We relied mostly on self-deprecatory humor. The reason this kind of humor works so effectively is that when the President himself laughs at the problem, he is in effect saying to the people, 'See, I can laugh at it; it's nothing for you to worry about.' It dismisses the whole problem by laughing at it."

Ronald Reagan makes himself the butt of jokes that highlight his linguistic limitations. He recalls with delight an occasion when he was governor of California and spoke in Mexico City.

> After I had finished speaking, I sat down to rather unenthusiastic applause, and I was a little embarrassed. The speaker who followed me spoke in Spanish—which I didn't understand—and he was being applauded about every paragraph. To hide my embarrassment, I started clapping before everyone else and longer than anyone else until our ambassador leaned over and said, "I wouldn't do that if I were you. He's interpreting your speech."

The Hollywood one-liner which is funneled to Ronald Reagan by gifted members of the Bob Hope and Johnny Carson stables, is often designed to kid Reagan's intellectual flaws. Self-deprecation is a Hollywood tradition. Jack Benny used to mock his own frugality. Johnny Carson kids his matrimonial losses, and Bob Hope deplores his Oscar-losing career. Reagan, a product of the same environment, uses the same form of self-deprecatory wit.

Self-mockery is sometimes useful in laughing away an image as a bellicose leader devoted to big bombs. Joking

about our expensive war machine can disarm criticism of big
defense budgets. Said Reagan:

> I've been getting some flack about ordering the production of
> the B-1. How did I know it was an airplane? I thought it was a
> vitamin for the troops.

Ronald Reagan laughs a lot, without scorn or mockery, at
the trappings of intellectual display. In introducing William
F. Buckley at a White House dinner, he said, "A word about
Bill Buckley. And unlike Bill, I'll try to keep my words to single syllables, or at least only two. . . ."

Reagan concluded by chuckling at the polysyllabic jargon
of bureaucrats:

> I've often thought when I've been faced with memorandums
> from deep within the bowels of bureaucracy what I wouldn't
> give to have Bill Buckley as an interpreter.
>
> You know, a fellow comes in, stands in front of your desk,
> hands you a memo, and he stays there and waits while you
> read it. And so you read: "Action-oriented orchestration, inno-
> vation, inputs generated by escalation of meaningful, indige-
> nous decision-making dialogue focusing on multi-linked
> problem complexes, can maximize the vital thrust toward
> nonalienated viable urban infrastructure."
>
> I take a chance and say, "Let's try busing."
> If he walks away, I know I guessed right.

Ronald Reagan has been criticized as a disengaged, cere-
monial president for a long time. He is accused of short working hours and long afternoon naps. Usually he laughs the
issue away. Of an especially busy week Reagan said, "I've
really been burning the midday oil."

Observers say he delegates far too much authority, most of
it to his chief of staff, Donald Regan. Said Reagan, "The
other day when I told Don Regan I was opposed to dictators,

whoever and wherever they are, he asked if he should start packing."

But there is evidence to suggest that the disengagement issue is a bit close to the bone, and Reagan resents the suggestion that he is a part-time president.

After the U.S. air raid on Libya, James Reston asked some disquieting questions. "What has come over Reagan recently to inspire this aggressive military response . . . ?" Could it be, asked Reston, that Reagan is fed up with charges that he is disengaged? Could the resentment be showing itself in bombers over Libya, bellicosity with Congress, and demands on our allies?

The question of Reagan's aloofness from his job remains a moot point. Even before his displays of assertiveness in the Mediterranean and the Congress, Ronald Reagan has been far from disengaged. Indeed, the dramatic changes in U.S. domestic programs and foreign policy during his presidency suggest that, without breast-beating and bravado, in his genial, laid-back way, Ronald Reagan has firmly established the American agenda and is very much in charge.

Chapter 4
Unchecked Anecdotes

> "Ronald Reagan is a master of distortion that generally contains a core of truth that makes it impossible or at least chancy to call the man a liar."
>
> JOHN OSBORNE,
> *The New Republic*

Most presidents collect jokes as avidly as a stand-up comic. Aides to Presidents Ford and Carter report that they each squirreled away a list of surefire gags in their wallets for use in times of need. But Ronald Reagan collects something much more useful than mere jokes. He collects anecdotes about real people, many of which never really happened.

According to his staff, Ronald Reagan will pounce on an anecdote reported in an obscure press clipping or related by an acquaintance, and incorporate it into a speech, without ever checking its accuracy. These stories are adapted and rearranged for the purpose of the President's rhetoric, much as an intriguing scene might be incorporated into a movie scenario by a screenwriter, because it adds to the humor or pathos of the script.

Reporters who cover the President regularly have formed the impression that he can be quite a master of selective distortion. For one thing, Reagan's anecdotes are peopled by a cloudy cast of characters whose names and experiences are never quite authenticated despite assiduous research.

Ronald Reagan tells of "a man in New Jersey" who was informed by the Social Security Administration that he was dead. Laughter and headshaking follow. The man proved that he was very much alive, and after an extended exchange of correspondence was paid $750 for his own funeral. The misty man in New Jersey, whose adventures went unverified by any Jersey newspaper, made a powerful case for the opacity of government bureaus.

To demonstrate that the government supports the undeserving poor too lavishly, and to show just how unworthy many of the recipients of welfare checks often are, Reagan relates the case of a Chicago welfare fraud who in the President's telling was pulling down $150,000 a year from her false claims. The woman, in the anecdotal version, owned two Lincoln Continentals and lived a lush life that a sheik might envy.

Demonstrating the fraud that barnacles our food stamp program, Reagan draws laughter and chagrin when he relates the story of a woman who was observed in a Safeway supermarket buying a fifth of vodka with her food stamps.

The errors of Reagan's anecdotal ways help him more than they hurt him. When Reagan cites an undocumented name, number, or event, it is difficult to disprove the story. And Reagan's manifest honesty is such that no one assumes, as with a Johnson or a Nixon, that he is telling a barefaced lie. Reagan's popularity and sincerity are such that he is always given the benefit of the doubt: He is not dissembling, merely inaccurate.

The mistake that Reagan's critics make is in supposing that he is presenting tainted anecdotes, while what he is *really* presenting is a world view in which facts are unimportant. The anecdotes amuse and persuade, which is their central purpose. Though these "facts" may be tarnished by error or exaggeration, the thrust is not the story but the attitude.

Ronald Reagan's view of the anecdote is more that of a polemicist than a historian. When one hears a story about

George S. Kaufman or Groucho Marx, one laughs and pays little attention to whether the story is true. Reagan shrewdly uses his unchecked or invented anecdotes not to amuse but to proselytize. And so, as if swallowing tainted food, we ingest the doctrine along with the laughter.

Reagan's defenders point out, with some justice, that presidents have always tended to stretch the facts. Lyndon Johnson related how his grandfather had fought at the Alamo, and when he was told the record did not bear him out, he protested that it was some other battle of the Mexican War and what was the difference? And when *that* statement was disproved, he muttered that the press was out to get him.

But Ronald Reagan tends to stretch facts, juggle numbers, and invent happenings to an extent that is excessive even for the political breed. He seems to fathom the crucial truth that his view of the world is more important than any sentimental devotion to accuracy. He is a poet of politics.

For years Ronald Reagan used anecdotes with dubious evidential support. His target was generally welfare chiselers who were defrauding the government and the taxpayers. There was a certain poetic justice when the public discovered a new collection of anecdotes about military chiselers who were defrauding the government and the taxpayers. These new anecdotes dealt with obscenely expensive nails, screwdrivers, and toilet seats and a defense contractor who boarded his dog at the taxpayers' expense. Unlike some of Reagan's anecdotes, these stories of Pentagon prodigality were buttressed by hard evidence.

Reagan's skill as a performer saves him from the downside of his anecdotal inventions. When Richard Nixon tried to manipulate us with faulty facts, he was trapped by his own guile. Reagan's acting saves him. He seems absolutely sincere about what he is saying, and doubtless he is.

Ronald Reagan is in his "anecdotage," say his detractors. Yet he is by far the most effective public speaker of our time, the most admired public figure, and like Will Rogers and Mark Twain, he is brilliant at weaving his policies into his anecdotes and his anecdotes into his ideology. Here are some of the stories that Reagan has used, with varying degrees of evidential support.

Speaking to the National Association of Student Councils, Reagan zeroed in on a frequent target, the evils of government paperwork and bureaucracy and their excesses.

> I know a teacher [said Reagan] who realized that the form he kept getting, filling out, and kept sending in asked some of the same questions over and over again, such as what was the size of his classroom.
>
> He got curious as to whether anybody in Washington ever read these reports, so each time he filled out the same old form, he increased the size of his classroom until he got up to the size of the Colosseum. But there was no protest from Washington.
>
> Then he went the other way. He started reducing it so that his classroom was smaller than a steamer trunk, and still there was no word from Washington. That's when he decided, "Why fill them out? No one's reading them!"

The President never tires of discovering horror stories about government regulations run amok.

> Let me tell you about this fellow in government who sat at his desk, and documents came to his desk, then he marked them for forwarding to the proper destination, initialed them, and passed them on.
>
> One day a classified document came to his desk. Since it had come there, he read it, decided where it should go, initialed it, and passed it on.
>
> A day later it came back to him with an attached memo that said, "You weren't supposed to see this. Erase your initials and initial the erasure."

Another unchecked anecdote was used to attack the permissiveness of our law enforcement system, which Ronald Reagan has deplored throughout his political career.

A few years ago [he said] two narcotics agents in San Bernardino, California, had evidence to get a warrant to search a home—a couple living there was believed to be peddling heroin.

They searched the home, and they didn't find the heroin. But as they were leaving, one of them, on a hunch, went back to the baby's crib. There was a baby. He took its diapers off, and there was the heroin, stashed inside the diaper.

Well, they went into court. And you know, the judge threw the case out of court on the basis that the baby's constitutional rights had been violated—for taking the diapers off without its permission.

Journalistic inquiry was unable to turn up this case in the records of the San Bernardino courthouse. But the story was certainly an amusing, cautionary tale about the coddling of felons and the excesses of our judicial system. Ironists were quick to point out that Mr. Reagan was usually more attentive to the rights of babies, but only during their fetal stage.

The diapers story has about it the whiff of Hollywood, as though it were the product of a group of writers seated about a conference table in the office of Norman Lear.

"We need a cute way for them to stash the dope."

"How about the diapers?"

"Great—and then the case is thrown out of court because they didn't read the baby his rights."

Ronald Reagan returned to his antibureaucratic theme with an unchecked anecdote he delivered to the Associated General Contractors of America about the evils of government red tape:

A fellow in my neighborhood not long ago was building his own home. He got so fed up finally with all the government paperwork that he pasted all the pages together, strung them up on two poles, and had a strip of paper 250 feet long!

Inquiries about Mr. Reagan's neighbor—he was living at the time in the verdant hills of Pacific Palisades—failed to elicit his name or the location of his property.

Some of Ronald Reagan's stories sound like scenes in a movie. After thirty years in the Hollywood cocoon, it is not surprising that Reagan tends to think in terms of "scenes." Many of his anecdotes and letters from the heartland sound like melodramatic cinema—a moment out of Frank Capra. It is not hard to picture Reagan visualizing these scenes and assessing their dramatic effect, finally concluding, "It will play."

Reagan's cinematic roots were suggested in a letter he told of finding in the White House mailbag:

[I received] a letter from a sixteen-year-old boy who said, "From what's going on there [in Washington], I'm sure that you're going to save the country for kids like me."

Movie buffs may note a suspicious similarity between the letter from the teenage boy and a line in the final scene of *Mr. Smith Goes to Washington*, as the idealistic young senator fights exhaustion and dismay.

Elizabeth Drew of *The New Yorker* recalled that the turning point of the contest for the 1980 Republican presidential nomination had come in the New Hampshire debate when Ronald Reagan suddenly invited all the other GOP candidates to participate in a debate in which only he and George Bush were supposed to take part. When Bush objected, Reagan captured the public imagination by declaring, "Hold it! I am paying for this microphone!"

The astute Ms. Drew noted that in an early Tracy-Hepburn film called *State of the Union*, Spencer Tracy plays an industrialist who is seeking the presidential nomination. In a nationwide broadcast, when his wife begins to read a compromising statement prepared by his corrupt handlers, Tracy seizes the microphone and halts the speech. Declares Tracy, "Hold it! Don't shut me off! I am paying for this broadcast!"

Chapter 5

The Gipper Versus
the Government

In no arena has Ronald Reagan used wit with more lethal effect than in his attacks on big government. Over a period of
thirty years—on the rubber chicken circuit as a General Elec-
tric spokesman and over the elegant menus of state dinners—
Reagan has lashed out at the bloated government, and his
perennial weapon has been humor.

There is an unintended irony in Reagan's demolition of the
bureaucracy. For he has used humor to ridicule government
in the eyes of the very people who have profited most from its
help.

What is particularly unsettling to Reagan's political foes is
that he is able to level his mocking humor at government programs at the same time that he praises the men who created
them, from Franklin Roosevelt to John F. Kennedy. To find
Ronald Reagan purring pleasantries at the Kennedy Library
one day and savaging Kennedy's social programs the next
leaves one glassy-eyed.

The world laughs at its tragedies, says the philosopher,
since that is all it can do about them. Reagan helped the
public laugh at the barnacled bureaucracy and rode their
merriment to the pinnacle of power.

45

American citizens have always had a certain disdain for the people who serve them. Reagan played on this distrust with biting humor, like a resistance fighter in occupied territory. His one-liners went for the jugular as much as for the funny-bone, attacking government waste:

> I've always thought that Washington didn't have the same problems other cities did because they grabbed hold of the fastest growing industry in America.

Humor is an unexamined form of debate. One does not dig too deeply into the logic of a Johnny Carson monologue. And this comic assault enables Reagan to fire away without having to defend his position on the naked field of reason.

One would have thought that FDR's response to the Depression had established the government's legitimate role in strengthening the economy and getting beyond such duties as delivering the mail. But Reagan's wit throws out the baby with the bath water. His antigovernment humor is like the rain that falls on the just and unjust alike:

> I would never accuse [bureaucrats] of ignorance. It's just that there are so many people in Washington who know so many things that aren't true.

Reagan has been candid from the start about his desire to dismantle much of the work of our last eight presidents. In playing off voter distrust of politicians, Reagan's humor implies that public officials are by nature stupid beyond measure, as when he talked of a mythical American city that had decided to raise its traffic signs:

> The signs were five feet high [said Reagan] and they were going to raise them to seven. The federal government stepped in with a program to do it—they came in and lowered the streets two feet.

46

Reagan is gracious enough to acknowledge that many of yesterday's obsolete programs were created by men with honorable intentions—they wanted to help people. But then he palms the ace, pointing out with the scalpel edge of humor that good intentions are not enough. They pave the road to hell . . . or Washington. Reagan draws volcanic laughter with an anecdote that has the fragrance of an ancient copy of the *Reader's Digest.* He tells of a fellow riding a motorcycle on a wintry day as the icy wind creeps through the buttonholes of his leather jacket. He stops, gets off, turns the jacket around, and puts it on backward.

> A little later [said Reagan] the motorcyclist hit a patch of ice and skidded into a tree. The police got there, elbowed their way through the crowd and asked, "What happened?"
>
> Someone said, "I don't know. When I got here he seemed to be all right. But then they tried to turn his head around . . ."

Reagan reserves his most contemptuous humor for the U.S. Congress, that pack of spendthrifts whose prodigalities he finds so hard to curb. "I've been criticized for going over the heads of Congress," said Reagan. "So, what's the fuss? A lot of things go over their heads."

Introducing Bob Hope he once said, "Bob's two great loves are entertaining the troops and golf. He just asked me what's my handicap, and I said 'Congress'."

"None of us really understands what's going on with all these numbers," David Stockman said in his famous confessional.

Because numbers are as confusing to the public as they are to the Budget Bureau, humor is an ideal means of dealing with complex subjects like the deficit and the tax laws. When the public is perplexed by a sea of graphs, charts, and statistics, nothing is easier to comprehend than a swift one-liner. If increased taxes seem a logical alternative to passing a crushing debt on to our children, numbers are less effective than a crisp zinger:

> Feeding more tax dollars to government is like feeding a stray pup. It just follows you home and sits on your doorstep asking for more.

When Stockman left government and wrote a book deploring the failure of Reagan's economic program, Reagan disposed of Stockman's few hundred pages of closely reasoned argument with a six-word gag. Asked what he thought of Stockman's book, Reagan replied, "I don't have time for fiction."

Reagan's critics say that in opting for humor over complexity, the President is approaching these matters in the wrong way: trivializing and distorting them. But then, public dialogue usually favors the comic over the complex. The public, with pressing personal matters to preoccupy itself, leaves burdensome details to its elected officials. If the officials choose to discuss these matters with the imprecision of a David Brenner monologue, the quality of public debate will suffer.

Reagan's supporters point out with justice that many of the programs on which his ax would fall have ballooned through the years. Many reductions are necessary. Some are urgently needed.

But they deserve more serious discourse than they are receiving, and comedy brings more laughter than light.

More and more Americans live in poverty. Teenagers, members of minority groups, and women suffer increasingly from job discrimination. Foreclosures of family farms are reaching epidemic proportions.

"That reminds me of a very funny story . . ."

There are times when humor is as out of place as a sandwich at a banquet. Those who criticize *Saturday Night Live* for finding comedy in such grim subjects as AIDS, drugs, and cancer should find the grim economics of the eighties equally inappropriate to the sound of canned laughter. Our government should merit serious appraisal and its goals should be free from ridicule.

Yet under Ronald Reagan it has become the custom to depreciate the federal government. Reagan has presided over its virtual dismemberment to the accompaniment of assorted catcalls and one-liners.

There is nothing secret about Ronald Reagan's agenda— hacking the bloated carcass down to size by getting rid of programs that should not have been created in the first place. And if humor cannot completely assuage the sufferers of this dismantling process, well, there are no gains without pains.

Shortly after assuming the presidency, Ronald Reagan went on national television and lamented the size of the deficit by declaring:

> Our national debt is approaching one trillion dollars. . . . A trillion dollars would be a stack of $1,000 bills sixty-seven miles high.

It took two hundred years for the stack to pile up sixty-seven miles high. Today there is another thirty miles on the stack. Small wonder that Ronald Reagan's detractors bridle when he cracks:

> Balancing the budget is a little like protecting your virtue— you just have to learn to say no.

Chapter 6
Terms of Endearment

"Like many people who are drawn to the performing arts, Reagan likes to please...to
amuse and entertain...."
ARAM BAKSHIAN

How is it possible to order cutbacks in programs designed to
help the needy and yet enjoy the love of your victims?

How does one eliminate farm subsidies and have the farmers attack your budget chief instead?

How do you order cutbacks in student loans and prompt
the parents of college kids to fix the blame on your secretary of
education?

The secret is being loved, and Ronald Reagan possesses a
charm and character that produce ample affection.

Like most past and present members of the Screen Actors
Guild, Ronald Reagan is a man who thrives on the affection
of others. It is axiomatic that actors love to be loved, and
Reagan, like most actors and politicians, long ago developed
an appetite for affection.

His speeches are sprinkled with humorous remarks carefully crafted to win the regard of specific audiences.

Reagan's public charm is formidable, and much of it flows
from his ability to flatter a particular constituency with well-
tailored wit.

He ingratiated himself with an audience of farmers with this anecdote:

> A farmer had taken some land down in a creek bottom. It was covered with rocks and brush and was pretty scraggly, and he went to work on it.
>
> He worked and worked and finally had a garden that was his pride and joy. So one Sunday morning after services he asked the minister if he wouldn't like to come out and see his garden.
>
> Well, the minister arrived and he looked. He looked at the melons and he said, "Oh, the Lord has certainly blessed this land." He looked at the corn and he said, "My, the Lord sure has blessed this corn." He said, "My, what the Lord and you have managed to accomplish here."
>
> The farmer finally said, "Reverend, I wish you could have seen this place when the Lord was doing it by himself."

Addressing a battalion of U.S. Marines, Ronald Reagan exercised his considerable charm with an anecdote that praised Leatherneck courage:

> There was a Marine detachment that was sent to an army base for some airborne training. The young lieutenant who was explaining everything said that the plane would come over at about 800 feet. They would jump and would then assemble with other forces in the area.
>
> When he finished, the marines went into a kind of huddle. Pretty soon several of them as spokesmen went up to the lieutenant and said, "Lieutenant, could the plane maybe come over a little lower, say at about 500 feet?"
>
> Well, he explained, no, it couldn't because the parachutes wouldn't have time to open.
>
> "Oh," they said, "we're wearing parachutes?"

Geographic flattery, aimed at the particular state that he is visiting, is a Reagan specialty. As a presidential comedy adviser expressed it, "One of the chief values of humor is to let the audience know that you know who they are and where they are."

Said Reagan on his arrival in Portland, Oregon:

Some of my hardworking aides recommended against leaving the Capitol and coming all the way out here. So to keep them happy I said, "Okay, let's flip a quarter to decide whether to visit your beautiful state or stay in Washington." And you know something? I had to flip fourteen times before it came out right."

Reagan employed a variation on this approach that combined geographical flattery with a swipe at a perennial foe:

Some of my aides recommended against leaving the Capitol and coming all the way out to Oregon. So I got them together and said, "Boys, we're going where the people think big and the sky's the limit." So they all headed for Tip O'Neill's office.

Texans have become conditioned to flattery from visiting presidents, dating back to Jack Kennedy's visit to the Alamo and beyond. Reagan did not disappoint them:

A young Texan boy asked a stranger if the man was from the great state of Texas. Seeing this, the boy's father took him aside and said, "Son, if a man comes from Texas, he'll tell you without being asked, and if he doesn't come from Texas, there's no need to embarrass him."

Reagan turned from Texasphile to Texasphobe in a single ride in Air Force One. After beguiling his Texas audience with one joke, he flew to Maine, where he charmed a New England audience with a joke that mocked Texas arrogance:

There was a Texan who was visiting a farmer in Maine. The Texan asked this old boy about his farm and what was the extent of his spread.
The old fellow said, "Well, it runs to that clump of trees and then over the hill and then down to the creek. How big is your spread in Texas?"

The Texan looked at him and said, "Well old-timer, some-times I get in my car and drive for an hour-and-a-half before I get to the boundary of my farm."

The old fellow from Maine looked at him for a minute and said, "I know exactly what you mean. I had a car like that my-self once."

Reagan's ethnic flattery is almost as seductive as the geo-graphical variety. In addressing a group of Italian-Americans he said:

When I think of Italian families, I always think of warm kitchens and even warmer love. One family was living in a lit-tle apartment but decided to move to a big house in the coun-try. A friend said to the twelve-year-old son, Tony, "How do you like your new house?" And he said, "We love it. I have my own room. My brother has his own room. My sisters have their own room. But poor Mom, she's still in with Dad."

For a leader whose public personality radiates decency and wholesomeness, Ronald Reagan has a surprising penchant for anecdotes with the aroma of the barnyard:

A farmer [said Reagan] confronted a Republican for the first time. He summoned his wife and said, "We've never seen a Republican before. Would you make a speech?"

Well, he looked around for some sort of platform. The only thing he could see there was a pile of manure. He climbed up on it and made his speech.

When he stepped down, they said it was the first time they had ever heard a Republican speech. He said, "Well, that's all right. That's the first time I've ever given a Republican speech from a Democratic platform."

He told a western audience:

There's one advertisement that I've never quite understood. That's the TV commercial about the cowboy out there in the middle of a herd of cattle, and the caption on the picture is: "Come to where the flavor is."

Reagan recalled the occasion when, six months after Richard Nixon assumed the presidency, Reagan had been asked why "everything hadn't been corrected yet."

> I told [the questioner] about a ranch Nancy and I had acquired many years ago. It had a barn with eight stalls in which they kept cattle and we wanted to keep horses. So I was there day after day with a pick and shovel lowering the level of those stalls where it had piled up over the years. And I told this [questioner] you cannot undo in weeks what it has taken fifteen years to accumulate.

Reagan tiptoed around another barnyard term in a speech to the American Bar Association, taking a swipe at the Soviet Union for suggesting the United States was looking for a pretext to invade Lebanon. Said Reagan:

> There is a non-Soviet word for that kind of talk, one with deep roots in our rich agricultural and farming tradition.

Despite the efforts of Reagan's imagists to expurgate his humor and lionize their leader, the President shows the same occasional affection for bawdy jokes as was displayed by Kennedy, Johnson, and Carter.

Bob Orben provided me with an interesting sidelight on the Reagan assassination attempt and the Reagan humor that flowed from it.

"According to the doctors who operated on Reagan," said Orben, "he came out of the anesthetic and told a dirty joke. This was reported in *The Washingtonian Magazine*. And the doctors couldn't remember what the joke was. All they remembered was the punchline. And *The Washingtonian* got in touch with me and said, 'Do you know the joke?' And I said, 'No, I don't know the joke, but I can reconstruct it for you.' There was only one way it could have gone."

Not surprisingly, Bob Orben's encyclopedic memory failed him when I asked what the joke was that the President had told as he came out of the anesthesia.

Reagan's appetite for popularity, a cultivated taste of many practitioners of his former craft, dismays his critics. Leaders should be willing to lead, they say, without the adoration of the electorate. Kennedy's *Profiles in Courage* described a dozen U.S. senators who had taken unpopular positions and weathered the scorn of their constituents.

But Reagan's zest for public affection may have its advantages, as columnist Mary McGrory has observed with telling insight. "A war ... would be unpopular," wrote McGrory, "and lucky for us, Reagan does not like unpopular things. Also, nobody else could take the rap for it. ... We should be thankful he loves being loved."

Chapter 7
The Genial Man

"He's a great actor. He does a great stage smile."

GOP SENATOR

Ronald Reagan's geniality is such a powerful weapon that it is able to shield him from the backlash that would normally be produced when his humor turns bilious.

Most men and women in public life have suffered a swift punishment when their humor appeared aggressive or insulting. Political history offers abundant examples of public figures who have been undone by their own malicious wit. To see just how extraordinary is Reagan's ability to escape the result of his occasional barbed remarks, one has only to reflect on the politicians who have shot themselves in the foot with misguided attempts at drollery.

Jesse Jackson's mocking description of Jews as "Hymies" brought him violent reproach—though his Caucasian fellow candidates were gun-shy about reproaching him for his slur.

President Ford's secretary of agriculture, Earl Butz, laughed himself out of the Cabinet with a brutal joke about the sexual and evacuative habits of blacks. Butz was so imprudent as to tell the joke to John Dean, the young man who had blown the whistle on Richard Nixon.

Reagan's controversial secretary of the interior, James Watt, drove the final nail into his own coffin with a joke in which he announced the appointment of an affirmative-action group that contained "a Jew, a black, a woman, and a cripple."

Vice-presidential candidate Bob Dole did irreparable damage to the candidacy of running mate Gerald Ford with his abrasive sense of humor, cuttingly displayed in a TV debate with Walter Mondale.

Ed Rollins, Ronald Reagan's campaign manager, put his patron in a most uncomfortable position by predicting, with leering distaste, that Geraldine Ferraro "would probably be the biggest bust in American politics."

George Bush, unaware of a ubiquitous microphone, cracked about his TV debate with Geraldine Ferraro, "We really kicked a little ass last night."

Not to be outdone by her ebullient husband, Mrs. George Bush joked that she would not characterize Mrs. Ferraro except to say that her chief quality rhymed with "rich."

All these strangled witticisms did their originators considerable damage. Angry, hurtful humor generally does, in or out of politics. But incredibly, when the darker side of Ronald Reagan's humor has appeared, he has escaped its consequences.

Speaking to the Gridiron Club, President Reagan brought gasps from his journalistic audience with the crack: "Perhaps we should keep the grain and export the farmers." This cruel jest came at a time when thousands of family farms were in jeopardy from Reagan administration policies.

In an impromptu mike test before a national address, Reagan joked, "I've just signed legislation that will outlaw Russia forever. We begin bombing in five minutes." (Mort Sahl quoted a Reagan supporter as saying, "I hope this isn't just another empty campaign promise.")

As governor of California, Ronald Reagan once alluded to American blacks as "strapping bucks," a reference as offensive in its way as Jesse Jackson's reference to Jews.

Reagan was sometimes inclined to ridicule gays, and once suggested that they could find a home in the Department of Parks and Recreation.

On another occasion he told an ethnic joke that was offensive to at least two nationalities:

How do you tell the Polish one at a cockfight?
He's the one with the duck.
How do you tell the Italian?
He bets on the duck.
How do you know the Mafia is there?
The duck wins.

Ronald Reagan is able to walk away from antic lapses that would destroy a lesser man. He has been so successful at making himself universally admired that callous jokes are shrugged away by an adoring public. This is the genesis of the phrase "the Teflon presidency." Satirist Mark Russell observed just how effective the Teflon presidency has been for Ronald Reagan when he said, "A group of demonstrators burnt Reagan in effigy outside the White House, but the effigy kept blowing out the flame."

When Ronald Reagan's humor is benign, h͏   house humorists point out the basic decency of the man.   harsh, these same comic mercenaries have a pl͏   uation:

"The wild lines like 'nuke 'em in five minutes,' " said Landon Parvin, "well, you can't take that stuff literally. Reagan would be the last president to start a war. He sounds harsh but he has a lot of compassion."

Parvin pointed out the crucial element of performance. The way Reagan delivers a line can take the sting out of seemingly belligerent humor. Questioned on the heels of Reagan's harsh one-liner at the expense of the American farmer, Parvin told me: "Sometimes his jokes are interpreted as cruelty. But when you see one thing in print and you see one thing in delivery, there's a world of difference. A lot of humor is attitude, and the President's attitude is genial."

Landon Parvin knows his patron well, and his proximity and access during Reagan's first term permitted him to craft comic lines that might sound mean on another man's lips. With Ronald Reagan, the anger evaporated in the performance.

"At one point," said Parvin, "when he was governor of California, the rest of the country thought he was a hard-edged kind of guy. But once the nation got to know him, they realized that that's not the case at all. They'd been *reading* the lines; they hadn't been *listening* to them."

The fact that is so galling to political adversaries is that Ronald Reagan is a very difficult man to dislike—even when his humor turns nasty. There is a geniality to Ronald Reagan that insulates him against criticism.

Some Reagan critics claim that this famed geniality is a facade that has been cultivated by the President—working in unison with humorists, imagists, speechwriters, and advance men.

How much of Reagan's geniality is calculated and how much of his wit is spontaneous are difficult questions to assess. But regardless of the exact percentage of chicken fat, Ronald Reagan doubtless comprehends the enormous value of his image as an amiable, decent fellow. The inescapable impression, however, by observers in both the political and the cinematic arenas, is that a great deal of the time Ronald Reagan is, well . . . acting.

Some senators and congressmen who have collided with Reagan in private meetings in the Oval Office tell a very different story of the presidential charm. It is a story much at odds with the legendary picture of Reaganesque wit and humor. Like a White House version of the picture of Dorian Gray, the private portrait differs from the public one in its capacity for anger and expletive.

One Republican legislator confessed that in his private meeting with Reagan he had seen little sign of the famous presidential charm. Pressed on the subject of Ronald Reagan's geniality and asked to confirm it, the senator grimaced, "Let's just say he's a great actor. He does a great stage smile."

Ronald Wilson Reagan has found humor an invaluable tool in flattering partisans and attacking foes, but it should not be supposed that he is alone in wielding this instrument.

Over the past quarter century, every president has found that wit is a weapon that permits him to attack without leaving footprints, to ingratiate without fawning.

It was not always so. Humor was not always recognized as such a potent device for public figures at every level.

Marvin Stone, the former editor of *U.S. News & World Report*, recently said at a dinner in his honor, "I've been in Washington a long time. It was a very different city when I got here. You used to find Velveeta cheese in the gourmet section of the supermarket."

Just how different the city has become was demonstrated by a glance at the various tables. The journalists were laughing, and the politicians had all taken out pads and pencils and were writing down the joke.

Part Two

JIMMY CARTER

"I am very grateful that my associate Walter
Mondale is here. I've done the best I could to
find something for him to do."
JIMMY CARTER

Chapter 8
The Reluctant Humorist

"I'd send in some stuff that I thought was great
and everybody else thought was great, and
Carter would think it was dogshit. . . ."
JERRY DOLITTLE

In the backseat of the presidential limousine, Jimmy Carter glanced through the final draft of a speech he would be delivering on a brief trip to the hustings. He winced at the jokes that began the speech and turned to his aide.

"If the American people wanted Bob Hope for their president," he snapped, "they should have elected him."

Despite Carter's distaste for humor and his view that it was alien to his personality, he brought a man named Jerry Dolittle into the White House to provide him with that dubious commodity.

Dolittle, in the words of Carter's chief speechwriter, Jim Fallows, "was a kind of genius with humor."

He had worked for various newspapers in the late fifties and sixties, ending up at *The Washington Post* where he wrote a humor column. His humorous work appeared in *Esquire* and *The Saturday Evening Post,* and then he went overseas for the U.S. Information Agency.

"Jerry developed a refined sense of black humor after serving as briefing officer in Laos during the Vietnam War," observed Fallows.

Dolittle returned from Southeast Asia in 1972. "I wrote a couple of books," he recalled, "and then went to work for Carter in the campaign, and followed him into the White House."

Dolittle was not recruited. Jimmy Carter felt no driving need for humor.

"I went after them," Dolittle told me. "I had just finished a book and had some money in the bank and didn't have much else to do. I always wanted to be in a campaign and there was one going on."

He called some reporters he knew who were covering the obscure Georgia governor and asked what they knew about the candidate.

"What they said sounded hopeful, so I started calling him and calling him. . . . Eventually I spoke to Jody Powell and he hired me."

Writing humor for President Jimmy Carter was not unalloyed bliss.

"Whenever the dreaded call for humor would come down," recalled Dolittle, "I was the guy with his foot nailed to the floor who couldn't get away."

Dolittle was the one that was called on to write humor for Carter's "impromptu" remarks as well as the comedic speeches for the annual press dinners.

"We—which really meant me—would hear that something was coming up. We knew the calendar pretty well. Then I would sit down and think of as many topics as I could that lent themselves to humor and then tried to make jokes out of them.

"Usually with that as a base, I would get together with other great wits of our times," said Dolittle dryly. "They would be people like Dick Drayne and Frank Mankiewicz."

Both Drayne and Mankiewicz, ironically, would later supply jokes to Carter's nemesis, Ted Kennedy.

Dolittle would grow acerbic at the comic contributions that

would arrive from Hollywood. The Carter administration's Hollywood connection was speechwriter Rick Hertzberg.

"We would occasionally get stuff from friends that Hertzberg knew in the entertainment business. These Hollywood writers would do jokes for Johnny Carson and they would usually help out."

Recalling the material that would arrive from the west coast, Jerry Dolittle grew petulant.

"They would send stuff in. It was almost never useful. They live in a different world out there, where the allusions aren't the same. Carson's guys do a lot of political stuff every night, but by and large these show business guys were off the target. Their references were almost all to TV and Hollywood.

"The stuff was just goddamn dreadful. There was one guy who had worked for Bob Hope—or *said* he had. He sent some stuff in. They were commercial gags, with brand names. . . . There's quite a difference between the television brand of humor and the political brand, and we found that out whenever we called on the west coast guys. . . .

"The Hollywood guys' jokes were all about Joan Rivers. Their cast of characters was different. Political jokes are intended for an audience that is presumed to be at least marginally politically literate. They have some idea what the Vice-President's first name is.

"Those Hollywood writers were so illiterate about that side of life," Dolittle complained, "that only the largest current events would impinge on their consciousness."

Whatever the merits of Dolittle's indictment, Carter seemed to be constantly betrayed by his inexperience with humor. One day a group of gags arrived from their man in Hollywood.

"We threw them in a Carter speech because we used to try to send him as many gags as possible, never knowing which ones he would use. So we got them to the President. Carter went ahead and delivered them all—and they were just awful!"

* * *

Jerry Dolittle's output would reach the President with little interference from intermediaries.

"Jim Fallows was the chief speechwriter and I'd give [my jokes] to him. He'd laugh and generally send them on to Jody Powell pretty much untouched. Jody would send them on to the Leader of the Free World, who would use whatever he wanted—which generally wasn't much!"

Carter's selections would often surprise Dolittle—a lament that seems endemic to presidential comedy writers.

"There was no great consistency as far as I could see. Sometimes something I thought was great would never see the light of day. Other times things that were awful he would use. There was no pattern that I could make out.

"I could never tell what he would find funny and what he wouldn't. I could never tell what he'd find terrible and throw away."

Of course, a U.S. president does not do a nightly monologue and so his need for humor is relatively limited.

"He's not Johnny Carson," said Dolittle, "and he didn't use huge amounts of the stuff.

"After all, he wasn't elected to be a stand-up comic. He wouldn't get on TV and do a fifteen-minute routine. And when he did, like at the Gridiron, the cameras aren't there."

Press secretary Jody Powell would pass on some humorous comments to the President, observed Dolittle. "Jack Watson, who was later the White House chief of staff, would sometimes send Carter some jokes. You would cast the net as wide as you could—and the President would cast the net too—and whatever he liked he would pluck out of it."

Jerry Dolittle had had no previous experience writing presidential humor, which was just as well since Jimmy Carter had no previous experience being president—no president does.

"This is something I had never done before," said Dolittle. "After Carter became president, an assignment came down that called for comedy. Jim Fallows and I were the only ones in the office right after the inaugural, so he said, 'Why don't you take a crack at it?'

"As shit tends to descend, it descended on me. And later I just got stuck with it."

Chapter 9
A Matter of Taste

"To a remarkable extent he was lazy and careless about humor—as he was about the rest of
his speaking."
SENIOR CARTER AIDE

Jimmy Carter's rise to fame and the Oval Office came on the
heels of the Watergate trauma, when the electorate was hungry for a man of honesty and decency.

A senior Carter aide observed wryly, "People were not
looking for a comedian for president at that time."

In the 1976 campaign, to the surprise of most astute political commentators, Jimmy Carter surged into the lead and
captured the Democratic presidential nomination. He was an
intense man—his detractors called him arrogant and self-
righteous. He was a not a man who leaned toward humor, nor
did he see much profit in bringing levity to his pronouncements.

Said a Carter aide, "When people tried to get him to inject
more laugh lines and bits of humor into his speeches, he resisted it. He didn't feel very comfortable with it."

"A major part of his appeal at that time," said a senior
Carter adviser, "was a very earnest, straightforward person. I
don't think he felt that the people were looking for a particularly urbane, sophisticated, witty type."

Whatever Carter's appraisal of the strategic value of wit, his taste in humor, on those occasions when he used it, was wanting.

For a born-again Christian who felt his own moral goodness was superior to that of the reporters who covered him, Carter's humorous inclinations were often surprisingly crude.

"He did one joke," recalled Jerry Dolittle, "that I would never have sent in to him. I think it was in Baltimore and he was in one of his periods when his public approval rating was below Nixon's at the time of his resignation. And the crowd was enthusiastic—perhaps he'd given them a big federal grant the day before. And there was a lot of applause and he used a line that he got from somewhere. He said, 'It really is a pleasure to see people waving at me with all five fingers.' "

Carter's lack of humor was described by a comedy writer and director who had served his predecessor. Don Penny, who had staged the comedic performances of President Gerald Ford, recalled, "I worked for Carter. I did several things for him during the Iranian thing. I went to the White House and contributed two radio speeches. I observed his lack of humor. I looked in Carter's eyes and I saw buttons. The second time I looked into his eyes I saw his feet."

One senior aide who requested anonymity remembered an occasion when Carter had been severely damaged by his poor taste in humor. Candidate Carter was a featured speaker at the Gridiron Club, and the assembled newsmen, the most influential members of the journalistic community, received an indelibly negative impression of Carter. The Gridiron Dinner enables ambitious politicians and curious newsmen to meet one another in a stimulating environment. The politician traditionally exposes his wit and perceptions of the public scene. The seeds of a decade of favorable or slighting stories are sown here as the cream of the media community—about sixty in all—form their impressions from the politicians' antic comments. These impressions are especially important when the speaker has presidential ambitions, as did Governor Jimmy Carter.

The December 1975 dinner was notable in featuring several of the men who were seeking the Democratic nomination for president. One of these was James Earl Carter, the obscure Georgian who was "Jimmy Who?" to most of the press.

Washington's journalistic elite would long remember the Carter wit as it was exposed that evening. He took the occasion to relate a bathroom joke of superlative tastelessness. It was a misguided attempt at humor that told much of Carter's judgment and sensibilities. It was the sort of joke that would not raise eyebrows at a convention hotel or in a baseball clubhouse, but at an assembly of Washington's most prestigious columnists and commentators, it ignored the necessities of taste and tradition.

The Washington Monthly, that lively and audacious chronicler of the Potomac scene, reported on Carter's embarrassing display of bawdy humor. What few chuckles the joke produced had been more mocking than appreciative. Said one journalist who had been present, "Jimmy Carter bombed out. He really showed his caliber."

The newsmen's distaste was not so much a response to the salacious story. Few journalists spring from the convent. It was dismay at Jimmy Carter's poor assessment of the audience and the occasion. Carter was obviously uninterested in humor and in giving scant attention to the speech, he was advertising a deficiency that critical wordsmiths could only deplore.

Reporters can be cruel in their judgments, and they contrasted the Carter performance and its lack of preparation with the immense care exercised by Jack Kennedy before he had visited the Gridiron. The Kennedy humor had been elegant, subtle, brittle, the perfect blend of brevity and wit.

In the days before JFK's first appearance at the Gridiron, all work had ground to a halt at his Senate office as the young senator and his aides assembled the witty monologue. Jimmy Carter, as an aide observed, "was lazy and careless about humor," and it soured the high priests of the press corps against him. They could never embrace him as they had Jack Kennedy and it would contribute to Carter's defeat by Ronald Reagan, a man whose use of humor was always felicitous.

Carter's maladroit speech did not make the wire services, given the Gridiron's tradition as an off-the-record forum. The public received no insight into the tasteless side of the born-again candidate who was on his way to a series of triumphs in the Democratic primaries. But Carter had fouled his relationship with political writers and done himself an injury that would continue to haunt him in the Oval Office.

Another example of Jimmy Carter's questionable judgment in matters of taste was provided by his comments in an interview for *Playboy* magazine. In declaiming on the subject of lechery and adultery, his language once again had the aroma of the locker room. Perhaps, as Wilde observed, the greatest sins of the world are committed in the mind, but in revealing his cerebral sins, Jimmy Carter caused a stir that nearly denied him the nomination. Said the candidate on the subject of infidelity:

> I've looked on a lot of women with lust. I've committed adultery in my heart many times. But that doesn't mean that I condemn someone who not only looks on a woman with lust but who leaves his wife and shacks up with someone. . . . God says, don't consider yourself better than someone else because one guy screws a whole bunch of women. . . .

A Carter aide recalled another occasion when the President's judgment about using humor before a particular group had led him astray. "This was the one time that he actually used most of the jokes that I gave him. It was a disaster. He was going out to Salt Lake City and he was being honored as Family Man of the Year by the Mormons. And his staff had written a speech, and typically they had written in: 'Humor to be added.' So I gave him three or four jokes and he used them all." Carter and his staff were doubtless unaware that Mormons do not raise their children to look lightly on the affairs of the world. "We were there in the temple," recalled Carter's sometime gagwriter. "And there were about two thousand people there. And when Carter told the jokes they just stared at him, absolutely stone-faced."

Another Carter aide recalled a Carter joke that had made both his aides and his audience squirm.

"I sat there with my fingers tightening as I listened to him tell this joke. The joke was about a guy who screwed up in everything he did. He screwed up in school, and he robbed a bank and they caught him. Carter continued a refrain about each time this guy would screw up he would say, 'Well, I'll get to it tomorrow.' And he wound up being caught because he was too lazy to run away. And the thing that was striking about the joke is that this was a nigger joke! Now, any southerner would recognize it. It was a nigger joke! He just didn't *say* 'nigger.' And I said to myself, Jesus Christ!"

Chapter 10
A Whiff of
Arrogance

"Jimmy Carter's idea of self-deprecating humor
is to criticize his staff."
WHITE HOUSE MOTTO

"Arrogance" is a word that was frequently used to describe Jimmy Carter, though many were perplexed as to what he had to be arrogant about.

Said a Washington columnist, "He was arrogant about his goodness, which he thought elevated him to a special stature in this world."

Said a former aide, "He had this chrome-plated, impervious, deep-down arrogance." He felt, said the aide, that his opinions were so manifestly correct that you should accept them without the blandishments of rhetoric or wit.

"He didn't put the time into the speaking process that he should have," recalled a senior adviser who requested anonymity. "He didn't do enough in the way of rehearsing. The White House speechwriting staff—in humor and everything else—was almost completely without guidance as to what he wanted."

A Carter speechwriter, whose prime responsibility had been in the area of humor, lamented the President's Olympian unconcern with matters of wit: "Humor is possibly the hardest

73

form of oratory and requires much greater care and preparation than your average tub-thumper does. Every word has to be placed correctly in the punchline. Getting one word out of place is likely to kill off the whole line. It has to be rehearsed until you're comfortable with it. But Carter would sometimes forget the lead-in to the punchline or forget the punchline. He was seldom reliable on anything more than a one-liner."

Arrogance is a quality that breeds a humor of sorts, but it is the humor of sarcasm. It is the humor of a man whose sense of preordainment assures him that he has been chosen to accomplish great things in the Lord's behalf. This attitude is not calculated to produce the humor of irony, subtlety, or joyous fun.

Chief speechwriter Fallows recalled, "Carter's private taste in humor was for the sarcastic one-liner." Jim Fallows, who has since become a contributing editor for *The Atlantic,* gave examples of the Carter sarcasm.

"Joe Califano, who was his secretary of health, education, and welfare, was renowned as a man with a sense of his own importance. I attended a series of briefings on various Medicare reform plans. And Califano went through these briefings using a group of charts, and at the top of each chart it said: 'Carter Welfare Reform.' And Carter gave a sigh and said, 'Joe, when you come in here with charts that say 'Califano Welfare Reform' then I'll know it's the right one.' "

Recalled Fallows, "He was more likely to discipline you with caustic humor than to say, 'You screwed up.' He'd use some kind of sarcastic comment. Sometimes a draft of a speech would come back to me marked 'C-minus.' "

The Carter sarcasm could scratch supporters as well as aides. During the '76 campaign he attended a Beverly Hills party held by screen star Warren Beatty, intended to solicit money and help from Hollywood luminaries. As he was leaving, Carter smiled wryly and said, "It's a real thrill to meet the famous people here tonight. I hope I don't get to know too much about you."

Carter needled his speechwriters one evening when he was addressing a Washington Press Club dinner. He concluded his humorous remarks by saying, "I told my staff I wanted them to prepare a talk for me to make tonight that was funny, and they didn't get around to it."

His sarcasm was often turned on his oldest political friend, press secretary Jody Powell. When some anonymous reporter called Carter a "cruel recluse," Carter announced:

> I have asked Jody Powell to find out who first used that phrase. He's interrogated all the White House correspondents and twenty-three White House staff members. If I find out who said it, I'll let you know. And if I'm not there, my *new* Press Secretary will let you know.

Carter would frequently turn his sarcasm on those who were closest to him and unable to reply in kind. Jody Powell was again the target during the Iowa primary after Carter, Greg Schneiders, and Powell arrived at an airstrip one morning and campaigned vigorously all day. At nightfall they climbed aboard the plane bound for their next stop. As the plane taxied along the tarmac, Schneiders realized that Powell was still back in the terminal. The plane was halted and Powell came racing along the runway. He scampered aboard the plane as an impatient Carter consulted his watch. "You know, Jody," said the candidate, "you've got one friend on this airplane—and it ain't me."

Carter could be graceless in victory. At a fundraising dinner in New York City, shortly after his inauguration, Carter said, "On election night when the returns came in from New York City and the former president, whose name escapes me—"

Carter's vice-president, Walter Mondale, was not immune to the caustic Carter wit. In a speech to a fundraising audience, President Carter said:

> I am very grateful that my associate Walter Mondale is here. I've done the best I could to find something for him to do.

75

Then he added:

> I would like to ask you to keep Walter Mondale from getting
> lonesome in the White House. He's given me a list of his proj-
> ects and wanted me to call them out to you. If you have ques-
> tions about the Concorde, Northern Ireland, abortion, gay
> rights, downtown parking—

Carter's sardonic wit was often directed at the Congress. He
felt his policies would succeed on Capitol Hill without the
grubby business of dealing with the legislators and conse-
quently was bitter when they obstructed his wishes. On a visit
from the President of Venezuela, Carter said:

> We were discussing the problems of democracies all over the
> world who are held back by the parliamentary process and
> congresses. We both agreed that these problems did not apply
> to Venezuela and the United States.

Addressing a dinner for Democratic congressmen, Carter
commented wryly about the problems the Congress was
creating for him. Said Carter, "I have enjoyed being President
so far—I tried to say that without laughing."

The creeping pace of the bureaucracy was the subject of
Carter's sarcasm on a visit to Egypt. While he was touring the
Great Pyramid of Giza, the guide told him that the structure
had taken twenty years to build. "I'm surprised," said Carter,
"that a government organization could do it that quickly."

James Earl Carter could exude a sardonic air about the
warfare in his own party. Speaking of motion pictures, Rosa-
lynn had expressed her distaste for crime movies: "All that
violence and bloodshed." Carter interrupted his wife: "But
you like Democratic Party politics."

The morality of his staff members was often a subject of
embarrassment to Jimmy Carter. For someone who had assumed a self-righteous posture throughout his campaign, the
moral turpitude of his closest aides caused discomfort. He re-

sponded to a question at a presidential press conference in a typically dry tone.:

> Q. It has been stated that you never held anything against people in your organization who were involved promiscuously with other women. Is that right or wrong?
>
> THE PRESIDENT. My preference is that those who associate with me would honor the same standard that I honor. I've done everything I could properly and legitimately to encourage my staff members' families to be stable. If there are some who have slipped from grace, than I can only say that I'll do the best I can to forgive them and pray for them.

Carter's pronouncements often had the ring of Billy Graham sermonettes. He preached often against promiscuity. "I have asked my White House staff," he said, "to protect the integrity of their families. So those of you who are living in sin, I hope you'll get married. Those of you who have left your spouses, go back home." But Carter's aides, to his chagrin, proceeded on the assumption that nothing succeeds like excess.

As Clark Mollenhoff observed in his trenchant book *The President Who Failed,* both Carter's son and his chief aide left their wives, and his senior advisers were often seen cavorting at wild Washington parties.

The social and sexual excesses of Carter's political family brought to mind the occasion when Larry Flynt, the editor of *Hustler* magazine, claimed to have a videotape of Alfred Bloomingdale's mistress, Vicky Morgan, sexually cavorting with three highly placed members of the Ronald Reagan team. Cracked Mort Sahl, "This cynical attempt to humanize the Reagan administration . . ."

The purported sins of Jimmy Carter's chief advisers never managed to humanize the Carter administration either, nor did Carter's wounding brand of humor.

The Carter sarcasm found its way into addresses to political groups where he might have been better served with almost

any other kind of humor, from self-deprecating to non sequi-
turial. Opening his remarks at a fundraising breakfast in
Newark, Carter said, "I'm always interested in coming to New
Jersey to try to comprehend New Jersey politics."

Carter even had a caustic remark at the expense of Benjamin Franklin. When Prime Minister Barre of France visited
the White House, Carter reflected on the first American ambassador to his country:

> Benjamin Franklin was our agent in Paris, representing the
> Colonies, and our own State of Georgia paid him an extra sti-
> pend every month—I think it was about $15 a month—to rep-
> resent us and our farmers, our tobacco exporters in France. He
> never came to Georgia, but he always cashed the check.

If Jimmy Carter was still bitter about Franklin's derelic-
tion, it can be imagined how the opposition of Congress or the
inadequacies of his staff would rankle.

Carter was not above turning his sardonic wit on those who
had helped him reach the White House. Returning to Roan-
oke, Virginia, Carter thanked Lieutenant Governor Henry
Howell, who had supported his candidacy and opened his
home to him. Said Carter:

> I've always been proud of the fact that when I first came to
> Virginia to begin my campaign and didn't have many friends,
> I went to Henry Howell's home, and he was nice enough to let
> me sleep there. I think Henry may have mentioned that on oc-
> casion.

It was not enough for Carter to accept Howell's support; he
had to deride him for exploiting it.

Carter's praise often veiled an insult. Lauding the man who
had defeated him in 1980, Carter said:

> One of the great things about President Reagan's personality is
> that he seems satisfied with the way the nation is doing. Popu-

larity has to do with the way you present yourself, and I must say I have great admiration for President Reagan because he does it so well.

Jimmy Carter directed some of his virulent gibes at his rivals within the Democratic party. Jerry Brown had been Carter's rival for the presidential nomination, and when President Carter visited California he remarked, "I got a personal handwritten letter from your Governor, Jerry Brown, but I decided to come out here anyway."

Jim Fallows recalls that Carter could deliver a dry, ironic line very well indeed. At times his wit would flash with ill-concealed impatience at a press conference.

Q. Mr. President, this is Jim Gill. Why has your Secretary of the Interior resurrected a bit of legislation enacted in 1902 that irrigation waters should no longer be available to any rancher who is farming more than 160 acres? The reenactment of this ruling is most archaic today. Farming methods are geared to production of food on a large scale, which is the backbone of our nation. Are you going to stand by and permit our most needed industry—the feeding of millions of people—to be scuttled by a misinformed member of your Cabinet?

THE PRESIDENT. Mr. Gill, I appreciate your very fair and objective analysis of the question.

The Carter humor was not very nourishing. It lacked the joy of Kennedy, the rustic richness of Johnson, the good-natured defensiveness of Ford, or the blithe bounce of Ronald Reagan.

"There are perhaps those," recalled Hugh Sidey of the Carter years, "who believed that there were a lot of laughs back there. Perhaps Jody Powell and Hamilton Jordan did have a lot of laughs, but I'll be darned if I can recall any. I found it wasn't very funny."

Chapter 11
Carter and the Press

"I'm not going to say anything terribly important tonight, so you can all put away your crayons."

JIMMY CARTER

Most presidents conduct a running battle with Washington journalists, but the antagonism of the Carter administration toward the media beggared comparison. Where the press was concerned, Jimmy Carter would speak in a humorous vein that too often turned varicose. It was a combative, wounding humor that the ladies and gentlemen of the press did not appreciate.

Carter resented the cuddly relationship between Teddy Kennedy and the Washington press corps, which reflected the residual fondness of newsmen for Jack Kennedy. It also reflected a growing distaste for Jimmy Carter.

The major irritant in the relationship between Carter and the people who covered him was that the President clearly felt himself superior to the reporters, in intellect and morality. Since love is the greatest aphrodisiac, the press was not enamored of a man who had so low a regard for it. It is said that a man loves that woman in whose company he most loves himself. The aphorism applies equally to press and presidents.

Unlike all the other American presidents of the recent past, Jimmy Carter did not work very hard at being lovable. Johnson inundated reporters with gifts, Kennedy gave them the greater gift of respect, Ford gave them access. Carter gave them a chilly stare and pious homilies. The press responded predictably.

Carter came to Washington an outsider from south Georgia, lacking the coterie of friends who constitute the Washington establishment. His staffers were also largely from the Deep South and brought the same loner mentality to the White House. Many felt they betrayed Carter's interests by failing to weave their patron into the social network of the city.

Given the hostile relationship between Carter and the press, it was perhaps inevitable that a number of barbed jokes would begin to circulate around Washington aimed at the President. Unlike the affectionate humor that Jack Kennedy had generated, the humor that Carter provoked was tipped with venom. One irreverent wag looked at Carter's toothy smile and suggested he was Eleanor Roosevelt's illegitimate son.

Carter was frequently ambiguous on the issues, and one columnist observed that he could never be enshrined on Mount Rushmore because there was no room for two more faces. Another newsman recalled the historical moment in Carter's boyhood when his father asked if he had cut down the cherry tree and the young Carter replied, "That's an interesting question."

Carter responded in kind to this press antagonism and his hostility was mirrored in that of his press secretary. Jerry Dolittle recalled an occasion that perfectly captured Jody Powell's resentment and that of his boss:

> One year Jody went to the White House Correspondents Dinner in place of Carter and it was a disaster. First they were pissed that Carter wasn't coming. They expect the President, and some big-shit press secretary shows up! So there was a feeling of sullenness. Jody was in a state of rage at the press at the time over a series of things. . . .

I worked on the speech [before the dinner] and brought it over to Jody's house. Most of the gags I wrote were self-deprecatory and there were some digs at the press. He looked it over. He was working out in his garden. He looked over my draft and said, "You know, we could sharpen it up and give the press more of a jab." And I said, "I don't know, Jody, how far do you want to go?" And he said, "Why don't you go back to the office and think about that some more and I'll fool with it here." So I went back and I didn't change it very much because I didn't want to be responsible for getting too bitter. I went back out there and he had done some more stuff too, and he read it to me. It seemed pretty strong. But I figured, they can take it.

Well, he went up there that night and gave the speech. And everybody knew that this was the kind of speech I was usually called on to help with. And Jody's delivery was very slow. He usually spoke in a slow, deliberate way, and this time he exaggerated that slowness. So whatever lightness there was in there drained out of it, and what came through was the nastiness, bitterness, and the real sincerity of his feelings. . . . I got more and more nervous as he continued. The correspondents kept looking around at each other and saying, "What is this shit?" At the end of it, reporters came up to me and said, "Did you write that shit?" And I said, "What, me?"

Distanced by their reciprocal animosity, Jimmy Carter made the press the object of his own sardonic digs. No reporter likes to be the object of ridicule, so Carter's derisive humor went unappreciated. On one occasion he acknowledged the antagonism of the press by saying:

When a president tells a joke, whether it is funny or not, people in Washington laugh. And my wife just said, "Yes, that is true of everybody except the press. . . ."

The adversarial relationship between press and president never left Carter's mind for very long. At a press conference early in his term, Carter said:

I've been to seven or eight news conferences, and I never knew there were so many White House correspondents before. You have my staff outnumbered ten to one.

Even when Carter tried for lighthearted humor aimed at a specific member of the press, a needle seemed to find its way into it:

In a White House environment [said Carter] it is difficult to separate fact from fiction, which reminds me of my good friend, Jim Wooten, here—the Erica Jong of the New York Times.

Later in the same press conference, Carter bent a sardonic frown at the assembled reporters and said:

I've had a lot of setbacks and a lot of troubles, as you know, and you've been kind enough to make those clear to the American people.

Carter obviously felt that the press could not be trusted to present the public with a faithful picture of events in the nation's capital. This attitude was apparent in his remarks at a reception of the American Film Institute, when he said:

The motion pictures have, in effect, painted the history of our country. I'm sure the movies don't distort history any more than the day-by-day life of our nation is distorted by the reporting of it.

Carter's humorous assaults on the press lacked the deft touch of the man who succeeded him. If Carter came at reporters with a bludgeon, Reagan used a rapier.

"I understand that ABC's been having some budget problems," said Reagan. "The news division's already laid off three hair stylists."

A member of the broadcast media who was often a bone in

Carter's throat was Sam Donaldson of ABC News. This news conference exchange between Carter and Donaldson displays the President's wit in the service of reporter bashing, as well as the determination of the press to give as good as it gets.

MR. DONALDSON. Now, after six months of looking at the problems and finding that the bureaucracy doesn't move as rapidly as you might have thought, and the Congress doesn't roll over as you might have suspected, what's your estimate?

THE PRESIDENT. Well, that's hard to say. . . . I think history would have to decide that twenty years from now, looking backward, rather than for me to decide after just six months in Washington. . . . As far as whether greatness or mediocrity will result from this administration, it's just too early to say.

MR. REASONER. Mr. President, one final question. We're sort of taking a poll, too. How do you rate Sam Donaldson as a White House correspondent?

THE PRESIDENT. I tell you, it's too early to say. Maybe history will reveal whether Sam has been adequate or below average or great. But after just six months, I've not been able to decide. I've put a lot of time in thinking about this question—but so far the answer has escaped me.

MR. DONALDSON. You've wasted your time, thank you. You owe about $10,000 back to the American people.

Chapter 12
The Fine Art of Self-Deprecation

"Goddamn it, we've self-deprecated ourselves
down to eighteen percent in the polls already!"
JODY POWELL

Political consultant Les Francis worked in the Jimmy Carter White House and knew better than most the value of presidential wit. "Humor," said Francis, "is one of Ronald Reagan's strengths. It was one of Jimmy Carter's weaknesses."

Francis has studied the various kinds of humor that are available to a sitting president and decided that the most effective kind is "the self-deprecating joke." Said Francis, "It makes people feel good about you. The ability to tell a good joke is useful in politics, but it doesn't convey as much about you as a good self-deprecating one-liner."

President Carter was slow to come to this wisdom.

The power of self-effacing humor to a politician is considerable. We like and trust a man who is able to mock his own failings. It is the perfect ploy. However arrogant or egomaniacal a president may be, let him laugh at his age, his wealth, or his golf game, and we are ready to turn over the keys of the kingdom. He stoops to conquer.

For a president of Carter's chilly mien, self-deprecating humor could be particularly useful. And though Carter re-

85

sisted humor in general, feeling himself unsuited to the role of stand-up comic, he was persuaded by those closest to him that self-effacing humor could be helpful. It could soften the growing perception of him, by press and public, as a distant loner.

And so, as time ran out on the Carter administration, the President turned to the humor of self-deprecation.

Jody Powell was dubious about the value of a president who was already in jeopardy attacking himself. Said a Carter comedy writer, "I remember one time during the midterm elections, we were going down to the Carolinas for a one-day hit, speaking in support of various candidates. Jody was there and they were working on humorous remarks for whatever the next stop was. The stuff that I did was pretty self-deprecatory in nature. I felt that was all you could get away with from the President. To use the tool of humor from a position of such power—it often comes off as nasty. Well, Jody looked at whatever the hell I was grinding out on the plane there, and he said, 'You know, goddamn it, we've self-deprecated ourselves down to eighteen percent in the polls already!' "

Despite Powell's misgivings, Jimmy Carter continued to take every opportunity to deride himself.

In the spring of '79, when Carter visited New Hampshire, his administration was coming under heavy criticism. A newswoman in Portsmouth asked him whether his daughter, Amy, ever bragged about her father being president. Carter said, "No, she probably apologizes."

Carter was even driven to laughing at his own special relationship with the Almighty. Before Carter's plane landed in a drought-stricken Texas town, there was a sudden rainfall. Carter stepped onto the slippery airport runway and smiled at the farmers who had gathered to meet him. "You asked for either money or rain," he said. "I couldn't get the money so I brought the rain."

The Georgia governor who had been known as "Jimmy Who?" ridiculed his own former obscurity. Addressing the Washington Press Club he declared:

I had been anticipating the Inaugural ceremonies and parade for a long time. I could see the burst of glory that would come to me the conclusion of the ceremonies, and I could hardly wait. We entered the limousine at the conclusion of the oath ceremony and got out on Constitution Avenue, and all of us left the limousine and started walking down the highway, and I could hear the vast crowd saying, "Look, look, look"—and I was feeling very good until they said, "There goes Billy's brother."

This bit of self-deprecation was a variation on Jack Kennedy's famous remark "I am the man who accompanied Jacqueline Kennedy to Paris."

Carter again resorted to the humor of reflected fame when in addressing members of our UN delegation he said, "In case you're wondering who I am, I'm the one who works for Andy Young."

The Washington press corps was astute enough to observe that Jimmy Carter—who would carry his own luggage and address the nation in a cardigan sweater—was making a studied effort to present himself as a man of the people. Carter laughed at this transparent tactic when he said to the press:

My staff is quite frank with me. I told them that I wanted to put on the image of a common man, someone who didn't have the accolades of the crowd and the homage paid to a strong and able leader. They said so far I have succeeded very well.

Any man who seeks the presidency must be extraordinarily ambitious. Carter laughed at his ambitions in addressing the National Governors Conference:

When I got through being Governor, I didn't know what to do. I could see the end of my term coming, and I didn't particularly want to go back to the peanut farm—and I talked to Jody Powell. And he said, "Why, don't we maybe go into the newspaper business?" I said, "Well, the only house I've got is in

Plains." And he said, "Well, we'll just start a newspaper in Plains." I said, "Nobody lives there but 680 people." He said, "How about the tourists?" I said, "Look, Jody, if there is one thing I am absolutely positive of, above all other things in my life, there will never be a tourist in Plains, Georgia."

Men in positions of prominence often find it useful to describe incidents of disrespect to their office. The humbling of the great is a favorite fiction to humanize the powerful. After a visit to Great Britain, Carter said:

> I went to early church service at Westminster Cathedral, and I nominated Dylan Thomas for entry into the Poets Hall of Fame. I felt sure that they would take action at the next meeting. As a matter of fact, the Bishop assured me they were going to do so. I didn't find out until I got back home that the next confirmation meeting is in 1999.

Jimmy Carter's ill-advised interview with *Playboy* and the admission of his secret lusts brought a firestorm of criticism. Here was a natural arena for self-mockery. Speaking at a fundraising dinner in New York, Carter referred to UN Ambassador Andrew Young, who shared the dais. Said Carter:

> Andy Young has helped me a lot. He made it clear that I was not the only one that gave a Playboy interview. And he pointed out to the Playboy people that I still was filled with lust, but I didn't discriminate.

Carter's gigantic smile was also a fitting subject for self-ridicule. It exploded on his face in a dazzle of teeth and gums. After it was announced that Carter's income tax returns were being audited, he announced: "My tax audit is coming out OK. The only thing they've questioned so far is a $600 bill for toothpaste."

Carter was not quite as humorless as he was often painted. Ted Sorensen, JFK's master wordsmith, pronounced Carter's humor "not bad, not bad. He often began his speeches before political dinners with a series of funny lines. And some of them were self-deprecating."

Then Sorensen added a lavish compliment: "They were very much in the Kennedy style."

Carter sometimes displayed his self-effacing wit at press conferences:

Q. Mr. President, there have been a lot of confusing statements from the White House on where exactly the United States stands in terms of Palestinian-PLO participation in a Geneva peace conference, if one comes about. Can you clarify this point?

THE PRESIDENT. I doubt it.

It is possible that Jimmy Carter felt he was displaying modesty when he insulted his kid brother—seemingly saying, "See what a simple man I am and what a simple man my brother is."

Billy may have preferred not to be a prop for his brother's feigned simplicity. President Carter never kidded his wife, his mother, or his daughter, though they were all fully as visible as brother Billy.

In the witty words of Stephen Sondheim in *A Little Night Music*, as the lawyer praises his wife to his former lover:

"The truth is she's really simple."
"Yes, that much seems clear."

The truth is, implied Jimmy Carter, Billy's really simple and his simplicity reflects my own. We are as plain and solid as the red clay of Georgia from which we spring.

But given Jimmy Carter's sarcastic sense of humor, Billy might have felt wounded by some of his big brother's barbs. He might even have felt, at times, that he was being made the object of thinly veiled mockery.

Speaking to the Washington Press Club, Carter referred to the mayor of Washington, D.C., saying:

> The day after the Inauguration, Mayor Washington called and said he wanted to thank me for restoring the faith in his city by walking unprotected on the streets of Washington, and by getting my brother back to Plains.

Carter twitted his brother's taste for beer and wine with lines like this:

> My brother Billy found out we were considering an ambassador to Martha's Vineyard. We had to explain to him that the name was derived a long time ago. . . .

When it was revealed that Billy Carter had received $200,000 from the Libyan government for the ostensible purpose of lobbying his brother in its behalf, the President used this as a target for his levity. Speaking at a meeting of the Southern Legislative Conference, he said:

> It is not often that a President comes as a substitute speaker. I realize that my brother, Billy, was the first choice. I understand that the Southern Legislative Conference couldn't afford him.

Billy Carter had developed various sources of income. In addition to receiving money from Arab states, he lent his name and promotional energies to a new brand of beer, cavorting in a costume made entirely of the lids of beer cans. He became a reliable target of his brother's barbs. Speaking at a Jefferson-Jackson Day Dinner, Carter said:

> My brother Billy has found another way to make a living other than growing peanuts. He can go to Canada and do a belly-buster in the swimming pool and make more money than he made all year on the farm. . . . When I mentioned that to Billy, he said, "Well, you forget, Jimmy, that I don't know how to

swim. . . ." But anyway, he is doing his share for the nation's economy. He's put the beer industry back on its feet.

Then Carter added ruefully:

A lot of people criticize Billy, but his standing in the public opinion polls is substantially above my own.

This was not actually the case. Billy Carter was a loose cannon whose aberrant behavior added to his brother's problems. As Don Penny observed, "Anybody who's got a brother like Billy Carter I think is very easily explained. He's a bumpkin."

Billy did not always take the mockery in good spirits. He was bright enough to know when he was being abused. "If your brother wins," someone asked Billy on election eve, "how will this change you?" "There's one change I'd make," snapped Billy. "If Jimmy becomes president tonight, I'm gonna make everybody call me *Mister* Carter for the first twenty-four hours."

Deriding his older brother's special relationship with the Almighty, on the day before Jimmy Carter took the oath of office, Billy said, "I hear it's gonna be forty degrees here in Washington tomorrow for the Inauguration. Jimmy must've been talkin' to the Lord again."

It is unlikely that Billy appreciated the occasion when Jimmy told a joke that called into question both Billy's literacy and his greed:

I was hoping that you would meet my goal and raise enough money to have Billy come out and speak next year. . . . I wish he could have gone along with my plans to involve him in the Government. I had it all arranged. I was going to reorganize and put the CIA and the FBI together, but Billy said he wouldn't head up any agency that he couldn't spell.

It is instructive to compare the often venomous humor that Jimmy Carter directed at his brother Billy to the more loving humor that Jack Kennedy directed at his own kid brother.

When Kennedy made brother Bobby the butt of his raillery it was generally wry and good-natured, reflecting the bond between the two. Responding to Bobby's reputation as the second most powerful man in government, when a call from Bobby broke in on an Oval Office meeting, the President said with a grin, "Will you excuse me a moment? This is the second most powerful man calling."

The humor that Bobby directed to his brother reflected the same affection. There was none of the envy and sensitivity that some observers found in Billy Carter's gibes at his more successful brother.

Noted Bobby as his brother began his third year in the Oval Office, "I've been associated with the present incumbent for thirty-seven years, the first few of which were slow."

When the West Virginia primary ended in a landslide for brother Jack, with Bobby acting as campaign manager, the latter's wife, Ethel, exulted, "It's so exciting!" Said Bobby, "I couldn't have done it without my brother."

And on the day Jack was elected president, the family was playing touch football at its Hyannis Port compound. Bobby was the quarterback and Jack went downfield for a pass. Jack dived for a ball that was well beyond his grasp.

"That's my brother," said Bobby, "all guts, no brains."

Carter's use of self-effacing humor was not nearly as effective as when the device is used by Ronald Reagan. One senses a genuine humility to Reagan, but one felt Carter's was a false modesty.

Why did the trick fail to play for Jimmy Carter? The answer lies in the words of Dr. Laurence J. Peter, author of *The Peter Principle* and other ironic speculations. Says Dr. Peter in *The Laughter Prescription,* offering advice to business executives, "By laughing at yourself, you can avoid creating the impression of being pompous or too self-important." Dr. Peter advises managers to tell humorous stories about their own mistakes. "Accept compliments with a smile or witty remark as though you are surprised that anyone would think you were outstanding."

And there was the rub. It was impossible to believe that Jimmy Carter thought himself undeserving of praise.

In addition, self-deprecating humor works best for a man of unquestioned power—a Roosevelt or a Reagan. It is a less effective tool for a man whose base of support is less secure.

Indeed, Carter's low standing in the public eye may have been exacerbated by his attempts at self-effacing humor. When a man who is not thoroughly in charge denigrates his own abilities, we are led to suspect that he may be right.

Chapter 13
The Carter Dilemma

"Look at our last few presidents—Nixon, Ford,
Carter, Reagan—a Mount Rushmore of incompetence."

DAVID STEINBERG

Jimmy Carter, to his grief, never comprehended the value of
wit to an American president in the television age. He doubtless recognized the solemn streak in his manner and tried to
soften it by smiling often as he spoke. But the chilly smiles
were unconnected to any humor in his spoken words. So the
smiles were never contagious.

It may not be credible to ascribe Carter's failure as a President to his failure as a wit. Yet his lack of warmth and humor
prevented him from retrieving his popularity when it went
into a long retreat.

Jack Kennedy and Ronald Reagan both had their failures.
Kennedy had his Bay of Pigs, Reagan his Lebanon. Yet both
had so won the public heart with their poise and sanguinity
that they were able to sustain their strong followings.

When gas lines grew long during the Carter presidency, he
had no reservoir of public affection to call upon as Kennedy
and Reagan did during similar stressful times.

How would Ronald Reagan have rebounded from a gaso-
line shortage? The invasion of Afghanistan? The hostage crisis? Not, one suspects, with anecdotes and one-liners. But it
seems likely that Reagan's upbeat tone, his optimistic grin, his

laid-back manner would have changed the chemistry of those
troubled years.

Jimmy Carter might be excused for feeling that humor—
calculated, manipulative humor—was irrelevant to the execution of the most powerful office in the land. Indeed, the
reader may be asking the same question: Why is a president's
use of comedy a noteworthy ingredient of his success?

To answer this question one must consider the electoral behavior of the American public, as opposed to that of the citizens of other Western countries.

It is difficult to imagine the prime minister of Great Britain,
the President of France, and the chancellor of West Germany
surrounding themselves with comedy writers who will supply
them with a steady stream of one-liners.

But then the citizens of those nations take their leaders and
their elections more seriously than we do.

In England's last election, over 70 percent of the electorate
voted. In West Germany nearly 90 percent. But in the United
States, when all the balloons had fallen and the posters
curled, only 53 percent had gone to the polls.

One is led to conclude that the difference between the
United States and most foreign countries is that in America
the public seldom finds any issue, program, or candidate that
is especially meaningful.

It was in America that a huge majority voted its approval
to Ronald Reagan, an immensely agreeable man. Much of
this majority disagreed with many of his positions and policies, yet swept him back into office, as Mark Russell expressed
it, "on a landslide of disapproval."

Many Americans regularly vote against their own interests,
if the candidate is sufficiently appealing.

Students of the presidential process have been studying the
commercial techniques of image making with great care, and
so have the successful candidates. Our selection process seems
to be unconcerned with such trivial matters as qualifications.

In pinpointing the best man for the job of president, many of us seem more concerned with wit than profundity, more moved by charm than substance.

It must have seemed bizarre to Jimmy Carter that to run the most powerful government in the world, it is important to know how to sell a joke. It would seem a laughable notion were it not so troublesome in its implications. It is Big Brother as seen through the prism of the punchline. It is measuring policy on the dial of the laugh meter.

When Vance Packard wrote *The Hidden Persuaders* in the fifties, we were stunned to learn how Americans, as consumers, were being manipulated by public relations men. We were shocked to learn how our opinions on the subject of cigarettes and soap flakes were being orchestrated by publicity men.

Today it is more disquieting still to learn how Americans, as voters, are being manipulated by politicians and their hired wits. Here our selection does not determine the sales of toothpaste but the path of the ship of state. With presidents you cannot return the unused portion and have your money refunded—except in the case of Richard Nixon.

Satirist David Steinberg has lamented the declining quality of our recent presidents. Lumping together Nixon, Ford, Carter, and Reagan, he proclaimed them "a Mount Rushmore of incompetence."

Steinberg's assessment may have been too sweeping, but during the past several years, many pundits have observed the steady deterioration of the American presidency—not in the power of the office but in the quality of its occupants.

Given the way we select our presidents, this is not altogether surprising. If the winner is to be the man whose one-liners win him precious time on the network news, whose self-effacing jokes win him an affectionate following, whose well-crafted anecdotes nimbly defuse every troublesome issue—then we are not likely to see a succession of effective leaders.

Ted Sorensen has observed that every four years the United States embarks on a cross-country marathon in which the entrants race about, leaping truths and hurling epithets. The marathon makes an ideal metaphor for our electoral process. But perhaps another way of picturing our presidential elections is as a lengthy audition in which hopeful comedians perform before vast audiences, entertaining them with an array of topical jokes. Their writers watch from the wings, one eye on the performer and the other on the ratings.

Certainly, wit and rhetoric are not without their value in moving men and the nation. But as Bob Hartmann, sagacious adviser to Jerry Ford, has observed, we should be wary of choosing our presidents for their oratory alone. There is a deep pool of preachers and performers in America, says Hartmann, and they are well equipped to give the public a song and dance.

It used to be said of Jimmy Carter that he was a generous man who on the occasion of a friend's birthday or anniversary would send a modest gift.

"So Carter became known as a man of modest gifts," said a White House humorist.

We demand many gifts of our presidents—wisdom and courage and leadership. On this agenda of virtues, humor should be very low in priority.

As Hartmann observed, "A great speech does not always indicate insight. It may only indicate a gifted ghost writer and a skilled speaking coach." And a skillful comedy writer.

Hartmann concluded that when a president counterfeits qualities of wit and wisdom, "the act corrupts both the man and the office."

Part Three
GERALD R. FORD

"Before I begin, could I ask a favor? Would somebody please keep an eye on my seat?"
GERALD R. FORD

Chapter 14
Without a Helmet

"Gerald Ford is a normal, decent, God-fearing man, but you can say that about a lot of people."

THE REVEREND DONALD CAREY

There has always been a linkage between humor and Gerald Ford, because to his detractors Gerald Ford has always been something of a joke.

Most of the jokes had about them the aroma of cruelty. Lyndon Johnson, who was famous for the malice of his humor, remarked that Ford had played football too long without a helmet. He doubted that Ford could break wind and chew gum at the same time. (This was bowdlerized by the Johnson imagists to "walk and chew gum.")

Jerry Ford was a decent enough man, but he was also unimaginative and inarticulate. As Richard Reeves observed in his astute book on the Ford presidency, Jerry Ford's lack of depth was more a virtue than a flaw during his days in Congress, since it protected him from offending any part of his modest constituency, which returned him to his House seat with regularity.

But then, given the vagaries of fate and Nixonian flummery, Gerald Ford became America's first instant vice-president. He then became America's first instant president. When these cosmic events occurred, Ford's chief aides realized it was essential to alter the public perception of this dull, decent man through a massive image-building campaign, the cornerstone of which was wit and humor.

Bob Hartmann was Ford's chief confidant and speech-writer. He knew better than most the deficiencies of his pa-tron. When Ford took the oath as president, Hartmann fed him a memorable and prophetic line: "I'm a Ford, not a Lin-coln." It was witty and accurate. Ford was no Lincoln. *The Wall Street Journal* observed, "Ford isn't a creative man. Rather he is a pleasant but plodding wheelhorse who speaks and thinks in cliches."

Hartmann saw the need to provide Ford with a facade of wit. So early in the life of the Ford presidency, he put in a cri-sis call to Bob Orben, the premier gagwriter of Hollywood and New York.

Orben had first come to Ford's attention when the House minority leader was invited to address the annual dinner of the Gridiron Club. Feeling ill equipped for such a display of wit, Ford turned to Barry Goldwater. Goldwater referred him to Senator George Murphy, the former song-and-dance man. Murphy referred him to Red Skelton, and the venerable comic referred him to the man who had written the cream of his monologues through seventeen years at CBS—Robert Orben. Orben's voluminous files of one-liners compared fa-vorably with those of Skelton himself, and Skelton's files over-flowed their drawers in his Rancho Mirage home.

Orben constructed a speech for Gerald Ford that shocked the assembled correspondents at the Gridiron. They had per-ceived Ford as a somnolent, witless congressman from Grand Rapids, not a satirist whose wit compared to that of Mort Sahl and Mark Russell. That evening, Jerry Ford glowed in the unaccustomed laughter and warmth of the press.

President Johnson had recently skewered Ford with his slanderous gibe about the effects of football on Ford's mental capacity. Ford replied with a prop joke that would have pleased Skelton himself. He said:

Let me tell you a little inside story. I've heard that President
Johnson tells his visitors: "There's nothing wrong with Jerry
Ford except he played football too long without a helmet."
Now I don't mind a little joke. But like so many other things
you hear nowadays, that just isn't true. And I can prove it. On
the Gridiron, I always wear my helmet.

At which point Ford produced his circa 1930 helmet and
struggled to put it on, to the cascading laughter of the press.
"This is really my helmet. . . . It used to fit. . . . Well, everything's getting a little tight tonight."

The Democratic speaker who sat beside Ford at the memorable Gridiron dinner was Hubert Humphrey, a man with an
excellent and exuberant sense of humor. Ford played off this
mismatch:

Why did I ever say I wanted to be the Republican speaker?
Matching me against Hubert Humphrey for laughs is like putting Twiggy up against Zsa Zsa Gabor.

There was a whiff of Hollywood to the Orben/Ford comedy—the invocation of celebrity names, the mammary humor.
Humphrey's loquacity was a reliable target. Said Ford:

Nat Finney [president of the Gridiron] told me how it would go
tonight. He said first he'd give a little talk, and next I'd give a
little talk, and Humphrey would follow. I said, "Who follows
Humphrey?" And he said, "Hardly anybody."

By now the reporters were stunned at the unexpected merriment of Ford's remarks. And Ford was enjoying the unfamil-
iar warmth of a responsive audience. And Bob Hartmann was
making a mental note for the future. Ford continued:

It's really tough speaking for the political party that produced
one of the wittiest presidents of all time—a great Republican
who always lightened his burdens with laughter and humor
and jokes—Calvin Coolidge.

103

Then Ford turned again on his tormentor in the White House:

> Hubert claims President Johnson is a teabag candidate—his strength comes out only when he's in hot water.... There's only one problem. Did you ever try using the same teabag for nine years?
> I know LBJ isn't going to miss a trick. Look how he's going after the serviceman's vote. You know, one of Bob McNamara's economy moves was doing away with paper towels in all Pentagon machines at every military base. On every machine there's a big sign: Press this button and you will hear a message from your Commander-in-Chief.

The laughter was flowing across the room, and Ford was aglow in its implied affection.

> Dick Nixon [Ford continued] doesn't have to stay in politics for the money. Only last week the Schick Razor Company offered him two million dollars just to do a shaving commercial . . . for Gillette. Dick's the only candidate who gets Five O'Clock Shadow on the Today Show.

So now, quite early in the brief presidency of Gerald Ford, with the new chief executive hobbled by his lack of charisma, Bob Hartmann recalled his patron's triumph at the Gridiron dinner and put in a call to Bob Orben in New York.

"Can you come down and give us a hand?" asked Hartmann.

"Sure," replied Orben. "When?"

"Like tomorrow," said Hartmann.

Chapter 15
The Orben Touch

"One of the problems with writing presidential
humor is somebody is always going to say,
'Hrmph! It doesn't sound presidential.'"
BOB ORBEN

Most political observers acknowledge Bob Orben to be the
dean of White House humorists, as the late Merriman Smith
was the acknowledged dean of White House correspondents.
The manner of Orben's rise to that position of antic prominence is instructive.

It started in 1945 when a teenager named Robert Orben
went to work in a magic shop in Manhattan.

"In addition to magicians," recalled Orben, "comedians
and jugglers would come in and they were always asking for
comedy material."

The shop and its young employee provided a unique commodity to entertainers: performable jokes.

Assembling and selling humor, Bob Orben became a respo-
sitory of comedy.

"I was eighteen years old at the time," laughed Orben,
"and when you're eighteen you fear nothing. So I wrote a
book. It was called *The Encyclopedia of Patter*. It was a success,
and before I knew it, I was in the comedy-writing business."

"There wasn't anything like that," said Orben. "There
were a lot of joke books, of course, but that is not performable
material."

Orben spent the next fifteen years writing special material for comedians and turned out a series of books that today number forty-six. Then television beckoned, most visibly the Red Skelton and Jack Paar shows.

"The business community started to get interested," said Orben. "They wanted up-front material, the jokes to get a speech started."

When the Skelton show expired, Orben returned to New York and the creation of special comedy material.

"One of my clients was Gerald Ford, who had become vice-president," said Orben, "so I became a consultant to him, and when he became president I joined his staff as a speech-writer."

Orben was a very special kind of speechwriter. His area of expertise was humor, a rare and elusive product. But Orben's experience in writing comedy for Skelton and Paar was not readily transferable to the Oval Office.

"Presidential humor isn't written the same way as you would write it for a performer," said Orben. "What we would do, [the President and I] would talk over what seemed to be the fun element of any given event. And we'd sort of agree on an approach, one that the President felt comfortable with. And then I would firm it up and put it into the structure that I knew would work."

In Orben's assessment, humor is a more difficult thing to create than rhetoric.

"One of my corporate clients once asked me, when his speechwriter was ill, could I do the rest of the speech, and I said, 'Sure, the rest of the speech is easy. It's the *humor* that's the hard part.' "

In writing humor rather than rhetoric for Gerald Ford, Orben found that he was able to avoid the destructive effects of the collaborative process.

"It's called staffing," said Orben wryly. "Staffing is what turns most speeches into oatmeal.

"Obviously, staffing is necessary," he conceded. "It's necessary that the advisers to the President get to see things. But I always had an end-run capability. And my end-run capability was an ongoing, one-on-one relationship with the President."

A president's advisers tend to distrust humor and try to protect the dignity of the chief executive.

"One of the problems with writing presidential humor," said Orben, "is somebody is always going to say, 'Hrmph! It doesn't sound presidential.'" Orben grinned. "The President would make his own judgment as to whether it was presidential or not."

Gerald Ford himself was never entirely comfortable with humor. Bob Hartmann, the man who knew him most intimately, said to me, "He had a handicap. He might not admit it, but he was tone deaf. He had no sense of rhythm. It would be hard for him to read poetry. He had no ear for it. And the same thing applies to the rhythm of humor. He knows what he likes but he can't duplicate it."

Orben became a cheerleader for his patron's wit. "Ford has a good natural sense of humor," said Orben. "It's a warm, around-the-shoulder kind of humor. It's not hurtful, unlike much of modern humor. It's not Don Rickles' or Joan Rivers' type of humor." Praise God for that. The mind boggles at the prospect of an American president ridiculing the sex life of the Soviet ambassador. Orben observed that for a powerful figure like the President, a gentle sort of humor is best.

Orben knew from his Skelton years that a wounding kind of wit did not play well. None of the banked fires of Skelton's hostility toward liberals and rebellious youth ever found its way out of his dressing room. Malicious jokes may draw laughter in Las Vegas, but in public life they are *de trop*. In his debut at the Gridiron, much of Ford's humor had a hard edge, but as Orben settled into the White House, he produced a more benign brand of comedy for the presidential speeches.

In the view of some members of Ford's staff, Orben did his job not wisely but too well. When President Ford made a substantive speech, the TV news shows, ever attentive to what they call sound bites, would lift out an Orben joke. A team of White House speechwriters might labor for weeks on a major address, only to see an Orben crack show up on the seven o'clock news.

"In the early days," recalled Orben, "there was unhappiness between some people in the White House and myself, as to all of the TV play that the jokes were getting. One of the things I stressed was that it wasn't just the joke for the joke's sake. Usually the joke humorously set the premise for the speech that followed. Quite often on the network news they only had thirty seconds to allow a visual on the speech, so the joke might get fifteen seconds. There was some feeling on the part of others in the White House that this was not appropriate."

Students of public affairs may be dismayed to learn that news executives and political leaders have formed a tandem conspiracy to replace complex issues with one-line jokes. But TV news is big business, and its producers compete for public attention by sugar-coating public problems with gaggery.

"TV news is a medium of exclusion, not inclusion," says Lindsay Gardner, the producer of the evening news at CBS's New Orleans affiliate. "Every excerpt has to be crisp and brief. Humor usually is. So if a public figure has said something funny, I'm drawn to that."

It is the conquest of the weak over the strong, the funnybone over the brain, the trivial over the vital, and entertainment over enlightenment.

Bob Orben and his peers were aware of this fact of media life; they realized that TV news producers made these decisions nightly, and that humor buys a president both air time and an attractive image.

Gerald Ford took office under difficult circumstances, following months of scandal and acrimony. His predecessor had found it necessary to proclaim at a televised press conference,

"I am not a crook." His aides had formed a grim procession, first past a Senate committee and then into the lockup. If it was an era of nightly Sophoclean drama, it was not an age of laughter. President Ford and his advisers realized that the times called for a soothing balm for the country, and the good-natured humor of a decent man like Jerry Ford would do the trick. He had a friendly manner, a likable personality, and what TV programmers call audience acceptance. Television seeks that likability and so do political parties. Both found it in Ronald Reagan. In the post-Watergate era Jerry Ford had to be reinvented and redesigned to satisfy a maximum number of viewer-voters.

Ford's humor, like his personality, had to be designed to be inoffensive. Warm, not cold; smooth, not sharp; a Ford, not a Lincoln; a Carson, not a Rickles. Ford would avoid telling the electorate what it didn't want to hear. He would speak to it in a friendly, nonthreatening way, tinged with amiable humor. Like Chauncey Gardner in *Being There*, he would be warm, wise, witty. Of course, Chauncey Gardner was not playing with a full deck, yet his benign charm would lead him to the White House.

Bob Orben was accustomed to writing for comedians who would entertain three hundred people in a TV studio and tiny groups around a living-room TV set. Now he was writing for a man who would commonly address twenty thousand people in a crowded stadium. This was a difficult setting for the delivery of humor, particularly for a speaker without a sense of the rhythm of humor, the timing of jokes, the tempo of punchlines.

"The very first speech I worked on," recalled Orben, "was his second major address as president. It was in a field house at a state university. And a field house with fifteen thousand people is a very tough place in which to do humor. You don't have eye contact with the audience."

It would be a formidable problem for any comedian. David

Brenner works in the comfortable cocoon of a nightclub. A president does not. Examine the physical setting in which a president speaks and you see there is a large gap between the first row of the orchestra and the speaker's podium. The President stands on a raised platform somewhat above his audience. The Secret Service dictates the distance for reasons of safety, giving little thought to the demands of comedy.

"The gap," said Orben, "is both psychological and actual. And humor helps close the gap."

Recalling that first exposure of the Orben presidential wit, he said, "President Ford was a totally unknown quantity at that point. And he opened the speech by saying:

> So much has happened since I received this invitation to speak here today. At that time I was America's first instant vice-president. Today I'm America's first instant president. The United States Marine Corps Band is so confused they don't know whether to play "Hail to the Chief" or "You've Come a Long Way, Baby."

"There was a very interesting reaction," recalled Orben. "There was a split second of silence, and then the place was up for grabs. Everybody was saying, 'Did you hear that?' It was the President saying he knew what a peculiar chain of circumstances had brought him to the Oval Office, but he was confident and he could refer to it in a joking manner."

If the Secret Service could do nothing to close the physical gap between president and people, they were admonished not to dampen the atmosphere for humor with their solemn looks. "President Ford gave instructions to the Secret Service," said Orben, "that you can do your job but you don't have to be so *grim* about it." Hence, when Ford was delivering Orben's jokes, his protectors were smiling along, like so many watchful Ed McMahons.

In the years since his White House service, Bob Orben has become the most sought-after political wit on the Potomac.

He conducts comedy workshops for political speechwriters in which he uses recordings of Jerry Ford telling jokes to various audiences. "I use a recorded version," said Orben, "of what I call a relevant joke. The average big joke in show business gets four or five seconds' reaction. But one joke President Ford told at Notre Dame got twenty-seven seconds of audience reaction!"

Paul Theis, executive editor of the Ford speechwriting department, recalled that twenty-seven-second blockbuster.

"There had been a lot of rioting on campuses due to the Vietnam War and Watergate. The dean of Notre Dame, Father Hesburgh, gave Ford a great introduction. And Ford told this one joke that no one understood. The press didn't understand it, the media, nobody. Orben had taken a couple of days crafting this one joke. He spent a lot of time talking to Notre Dame students. It seems the university had a bus that would take students across the state line where they could buy booze at eighteen. And they called the bus 'The Quickie.' The university frowned on the practice. And so Ford said:

I have always been impressed by the outstanding record of the students of the University of Notre Dame. You have always been leaders in academic achievement, in social concerns, in sports prowess, and now, once again, you are blazing new paths in the development of new concepts in mass transportation. Some communities have the mono-rail, some have the subway, Notre Dame has the quickie.

Said Orben: "There were twenty-seven seconds of laughter and applause—we timed it. The students were cheering and stamping their feet. From then on in the speech, Ford could do no wrong." Forgotten was Vietnam. Forgotten was Watergate. Just one joke, tied to whiskey and sex, and the audience responded with twenty-seven seconds of pandemonium. Small wonder that Gerald Ford plighted his troth with Robert Orben.

Whatever the temperamental excesses of Red Skelton and Jack Paar, they could always be depended upon to deliver a joke as it was written. Alas, the same could not be said of Gerald Ford, whose background as a college football hero, male model, and House minority leader did not equip him for the work of a stand-up comic. Thus, Bob Orben suffered inordinately as he traveled with the President and watched him mangle his carefully tailored prose.

One national magazine referred to him as "Jerry the joke killer." As the principal supplier of wit, Bob Orben was careful to conceal his pain. Orben was once described by *The New Republic* as "a professional gagster who with his bald head and solemn mien resembles a monk in flight from a monastery." Some newsmen opined that Ford's jokes were not worth killing; they were dead on arrival. But in justice, most had the deft Orben touch and deserved a better fate. Here is one of the Orben anecdotes as Ford delivered it:

> As I was walking through the lobby a very friendly lady came up to me, shook my hand, and said, "I know you from somewhere. But I just can't remember your name." So in a friendly way I tried to help her out. I said, "I am Jerry Ford." She said, "No, but you're closer."

As any inveterate sitcom watcher will perceive, the correct punchline is "No, but you're close." The expected laughter did not materialize, and the President, lacking a sense of rhythm, timing, and humor, felt betrayed.

Ford undermined his humor once again when he spoke at a luncheon of the National Athletic Association. Said President Ford:

> I want you to know that I feel very much at home here today, because if you stop to think about it, the athletic director of any college and the President of the United States have a great deal in common: We both need the talent, we both need the co-

operation of others, we both get a lot of criticism, and we both have a certain lack of performance in our jobs.

The correct word in the punchline was not "performance" but "permanence." Hardly a twenty-seven-second joke, but deserving a better fate.

Orben winced at the mistake and determined to guard against future ones with more rehearsals.

There was also another remedy, what professional comedians call savers. Orben gave the President a special card to paste into his speech book. It bore a line to use if ever Ford botched a joke. It read: "I told my wife that I knew this speech backwards, and I think that is the way I am doing it." Ford liked the line so much that he would often botch a line in order to use it.

On one campaign swing, Jerry Ford told an extended anecdote that Orben had crafted from an actual occurrence. Unlike much of Orben's output, it had the charm of verisimilitude. Ford's daughter Susan and his personal photographer, David Hume Kennerly, had bought the President a dog and this produced a situation that in Orben's hands made for a funny, self-deprecating story. To the presidential press it was a tedious, interminable tale, but Ford liked the story and told it repeatedly for nine days at dozens of stops as he campaigned for old friends in the Congress. Perhaps he intended to keep telling it until he got it right. Said Ford:

We have a new addition to the White House. My daughter Susan and our new White House photographer Dave Kennerly got together and surprised me with a beautiful golden retriever. Let me tell you how Susan and Dave acquired this new dog for the White House. They called up a highly recommended kennel and said that they wanted to buy a golden retriever puppy. The owner said that was fine, but who will the owner be? And they said it was a surprise and they wanted to keep it secret. Well, the owner said he didn't sell dogs that way. He would have to know whether the dog was going to have a

113

good home. So Susan and Dave said to the kennel owner that the parents were friendly, they were middle-aged, and they lived in a big, white house with a fence around it. The kennel owner said that was good, but do they own or rent? Well, Dave and Susan were a little perplexed with that question, and they thought for a moment and said, "Well, I guess you might call it public housing." The kennel owner said, well that was all right. But he said the dog was healthy and was going to eat a lot. Does the father have a steady job? Well, they were stuck for an answer to that one.

As the President related the story at each stop, Bob Orben could be observed silently reciting the story along with him, perhaps reflecting on how the story might be further prolonged.

In his book *The President: A Week in the Life of Gerald Ford,* John Hersey recorded an exchange between Orben and Ford that was instructive. Orben was rehearsing Ford in a speech he had written for a dinner of the Radio and Television Correspondents Association.

FORD. [reading] I have only one thing to say about a program that calls for me to follow Bob Hope—it's ridiculous. Bob Hope has enormous stage presence, superb comedy timing, and the finest writers in the business. I'm standing here in a rented tuxedo—with three jokes from Earl Butz!

ORBEN. I've been playing the tapes of your speeches. Your timing at the Alfalfa Club was fine—conversational. But other times you tend to be a little slow. Whenever you're doing humor, don't pause in a sentence. Watch Hope. You'll see he really punches through a line. Don't pause.

The President tried the line again and Orben nodded.

ORBEN. That's better.

FORD. Is it moving?

ORBEN. You're moving right along . . .

FORD. [continuing] This has really been a very exciting week in Washington. Particularly in the Congress. On Monday, Carl Albert picked up Bella Abzug's hat by mistake, put it on, and disappeared for three days.

ORBEN. Very good.

FORD. If I get a laugh—would it be a good idea to gesture, as if I'm putting on a big hat?

ORBEN. I don't think it's necessary. They'll be getting a visual picture. But if you're more comfortable doing it that way—

FORD. It's a little demonstrative.

ORBEN. It wouldn't hurt.

Chapter 16
Hollywood on the Potomac

"In all the time I'd known President Ford, he
and I had engaged in good-natured kidding
about his long, sometimes dull speeches."
DAVID HUME KENNERLY

David Kennerly, the Pulitzer Prize–winning *Time* photographer who had joined the Ford administration as the official White House photographer, had a close relationship with Jerry Ford. Perhaps Ford saw himself as a young man in the puckish Kennerly. Whatever the reason, the photographer was permitted an access and an intimacy with the President that was rare indeed.

Perhaps that is why, as the White House geared up for the election campaign against Jimmy Carter, Kennerly had the temerity to write an outspoken memo to his boss deploring his leaden speaking style and pleading with him to liven up the act. Wrote Kennerly:

I can't sit back and watch you go down the tube without saying anything. . . . Your speeches are usually long, boring, and filled with rhetoric that turns people off. I've seen advance men literally cry when ten or fifteen minutes after you started speaking the people would start leaving. . . . Your speechwriting department has driven mediocrity to new heights. If this were my opinion alone, I'd say perhaps I could be wrong. It's not. It's universal.... You need a bunch of new, hungry, energetic young people....

Kennerly's audacity led to some changes. The New York ad agency of Ogilvy and Mather was brought in to produce a new series of TV commercials, and a man named Don Penny was hired to produce them.

Penny was an energetic fellow who had started out writing and directing comedy in Hollywood, then moved to New York to direct TV commercials. His exuberance would enliven Ford's delivery at the GOP convention and on the campaign trail as dramatically as had the comedy of Bob Orben. During this critical period, Orben had been shunted into an administrative position, editing the President's speeches and messages. He lacked the time to devote to humor, so Penny's influence on the Ford performance was critical during the election campaign.

Orben soldiered on in his new capacity but felt the change was a mistake. "President Ford wanted to put me in charge of the speechwriting operation," said Orben grimly. "I felt I would be more valuable as a writer of humor. Carter had very little sense of humor, but I was up to my ears in paperwork. So we didn't respond with the humor we should have. I always felt very bad about that, because I was putting in eighteen-hour days and there was no longer the quiet time to sit down and write humor."

With Orben devoted to editing boilerplate prose, the President's humor—in both words and delivery—was to be dramatically influenced by Don Penny, the protean, hyperactive product of advertising and show business.

Penny's welcome at the White House was not especially warm. "I was put down for coming from Hollywood," recalled Penny. "And I said to the guys in Washington, let me tell you something. Hollywood has historically always done much better than Washington. And they said, what do you

117

mean by that? And I said, when it comes to communicating, Warner Brothers has always done a lot better than the White House."

Penny's principal antagonist had been Bob Hartmann, Ford's chief aide and speechwriter. Penny remembered Hartmann with some bitterness. "He didn't want me there," said Penny. "He was away, and when he returned and found they had hired me, he almost had apoplexy. I used to call him the snow toad, because he used to remind me of this great big frog and all he could do was make this croaking noise. At one meeting he said to me, 'I don't think we need you here, kid. You're outta your league and I think you should get outta here.' At which point I said, 'Bob, you know what? I really got a problem. Let me explain what the problem is. There's only one thing that really gets me crazy and that's a bully.' "

Penny recalled with pleasure the summons he had received from Dave Kennerly. The two had first met in Vietnam and had stayed in touch. Then early in the Ford-Carter campaign, Kennerly had taken the shuttle from Washington to New York and proceeded to Penny's apartment.

"I was in my bathtub," said Penny. "Kennerly said to me, quote, 'Don, the President needs you.' Now, if you don't think that night I got out of bed and I looked out at the Hudson River and I said, 'My President needs me!' " Penny began to whistle "The Battle Hymn of the Republic." "If you don't think I was so proud, and so scared . . ."

His first meeting with Gerald Ford had a seismic effect on Don Penny. "What I liked about Jerry Ford was his solid base. He was just as real as could be. And his sense of humor was best when he was relaxed. Most people don't work to audiences very well. It's not a normal thing to want to get in front of a bunch of people and make them laugh. Most people don't have that need."

So Don Penny set out to take a relaxed former congressman from Grand Rapids and give him the ability to make people laugh.

"I came from a different place," said Penny. "I'm a kid from Brooklyn and I've been hustling since I was four years old. The bottom line for me was, hey kid, there aren't too many people who are going to stand there and support you. You'd better do it by yourself."

The sincerity of President Gerald Ford made an indelible impression on Don Penny. "I meet this guy after forty years of being a huckster, a writer, a comedian, a producer, a director—and all of a sudden here's a guy who just plain ain't full of shit."

David Kennerly had brought Penny to the President and Penny gave his assessment of the feisty young photographer: "Kennerly has the instincts of a con man and the morals of a priest. And that's what kindled my relationship with David. Because I think outwardly David thought of me as this New York hype guy, and then he found who I really was—I was somebody who was just dying for an opportunity to *believe* in somebody."

Penny's years in Hollywood had left him cynical about the morality of the film and TV capital. In Washington he found a sense of ethics that was not apparent to him in southern California. "I found that there was morality, that there were people who were devoted. And that's why I came to Washington. In California the basic talent is singin' and dancin'. In Washington the basic talent is loyalty. And I ain't found too much anywhere else." Recalling his struggles with television programmers, Penny said, "For the first time in my fifty years, I'd found a place where I made friends who don't last just thirteen weeks."

The Ford White House was a salutary change for Don Penny. "When I was out in California," he reflected, "the mode of travel was fear. And most people have made a religion out of it. I was never real comfortable out in California, because coming from Brooklyn, I knew bullshit from sincerity."

Don Penny was moved by Ford's basic honesty. He speaks

of it with born-again fervor: "I went down to the White House and my head said, 'I'm gonna help this guy.' And you wanna know something? I did. And you wanna know something else? He *still* doesn't know what I did."

And what did Don Penny do for Gerald Ford?

"I helped him in the way a director helps any performer. I said to him that the written word in a speech has to be translated into dialogue. In Hollywood we have something that they call a dialogue director. Somebody writes a script and then some motherfucker puts it into dialogue. And when you write, in this case for Jerry Ford, I had to be blunt with him, and I said, 'Mr. President, in 1927 William Wellman met a guy named Gary Cooper, a cowboy kid who didn't know how to talk. And Wellman sized him up pretty quick and taught him what I call the Steve McQueen Syndrome, which is don't talk, listen. And all the shots that Wellman made of Gary Cooper were reaction shots. You saw the man's vulnerability, his sensitivity, his warmth, his reality—and you *loved* him. . . .'

"So I said to Jerry Ford, 'Mr. President, you basically have as much ability to make a presidential speech as anybody selling shoes. And it would be my advice to you to understand that you are at best an eight-minute speaker.' Because he was then doin' forty-five-minute speeches. And Kennerly was sayin', 'How do you cut it down?' My answer is—you make him *stop*. Because between you and me, Lincoln did it in three and a half minutes. And five paragraphs. And if you can't tell somebody what you want to tell them in three and a half minutes, you never tell 'em! So my bottom line in helping Jerry Ford was in teaching him how to edit himself. Two, to turn rhetoric into conversation. And three, to get up there and relate to an audience in a much more informal manner. So that instead of making a speech, he did a *talk*. And most of all, I taught him to stop talking and start *listening*. 'Do five minutes, Mr. President, and then start questions and answers. And start talking *with* the people and not *at* them.' And goddamn it, the difference was absolutely incredible!"

Penny moved a videotape machine into the Oval Office and taped the President delivering one of his speeches. Penny goaded, cajoled, and refined, giving his new client the mixture of praise and criticism that Hollywood directors have been doling out since D. W. Griffith. Penny had Ford videotape the same speech five times, playing it back to show Ford his deficiencies and his improvement.

Penny had his work cut out for him. Ford was not the ideal subject for a director of speech. He had no sense of vocal rhythm. Cadence eluded him. It took determination and grueling rehearsal before he could deliver an effective address. An examination of the original drafts of his speeches at the Ford Library reveals a thicket of slashes for pauses, underlines for emphasis, marginal notes like "smile," "wait," "slow," and "emphasis." The abundant reminders tell their own story. But Don Penny was not discouraged.

"As far as I was concerned," said Penny, "within three weeks there was a vast change. And over the months I was there, when he finally went to the convention and when he did the acceptance speech, it was originally fifty-six minutes, and we cut it to thirty-six. And I *paced* it. I made him understand you can't keep it up for thirty-six minutes. It's like ten rounds in the ring. It's like you're playing football, and he said, 'Oh really?' and I said, 'Yeah. You got twelve minutes to make 'em listen, you got twelve minutes to pull back and let 'em come to you, and the last twelve minutes you're headin' down the track with the baton in your hand, and you're gonna have to win that race!' "

Despite the pained expressions of professional politicians and the doubt and antagonism of Bob Hartmann, Penny was having his effect. It was generally acknowledged that Jerry Ford's speech accepting the presidential nomination was an extraordinary performance. It was widely praised for its dramatic delivery and sent shock waves through the enemy camp.

"We did fifteen videotapes!" recalled Penny. "And he

started understanding what I was talkin' about. Because I played Jerry Ford in the first tapes. I did the whole speech so he could see what I meant in regards to pacing. I did the speech! I always do this with some sort of comedy to get people laughin'. I said, 'Mr. President, you have a speech pattern. You talk like this.' " Penny thereupon produced a sound like a seventy-eight-RPM record being played at thirty-three—a moaning, ashmatic wheeze. " 'While Jimmy Carter is something like this.' " And Penny produced a sound like a neurotic Bugs Bunny. "Ford started to laugh, and I said, 'Now you understand what I'm tryin' to say when I say I'm gonna write a speech for *you*—that is your words and your pacing, and basically your execution. And I'll be sittin' there playin' Jiminy Cricket to your Pinocchio.' And he said, 'Well, I like that.' "

Penny has reflected on those heady hours spent in the presidential presence. "You know," he said, "we had long conversations and President Ford said to me, 'Don, tell me, why are German Jews so goddamn smart?'

"Jerry Ford was willing to let me do Brer Rabbit to his Brer Bear. Ford let me climb all over him. And at one point Ford looked at me and Kennerly and said, 'I really don't understand why I don't kill the two of you.' "

Gerald Ford lost the general election to Jimmy Carter and moved to California. But Don Penny remained in Washington. His talent at enlivening political speeches had attracted a wide following in the Republican party.

"What I did for Ford," said Penny, "I did the same thing at the Republican National Convention this past August." This was the convention that renominated Ronald Reagan. "I did this for forty-six speakers including Jeane Kirkpatrick, and rewrote and edited almost fifty speeches. I took Laxalt's speech of an hour and cut it down to thirty-two minutes. He couldn't believe it. And he said, 'How did you do that?' And I said, 'That's what I do.' "

Don Penny's current partnership with Landon Parvin

numbers among its clients the most famous men and women in Washington.

"Landon and I," declared Penny, "are already getting involved in the '86 and '88 elections. And we've been asked delightfully by every major candidate to work for them. We're presently negotiating a deal with Howard Baker to do a radio show for him—three a week. Because I like him—I like him as a man. He's a lot like Jerry Ford. And he too is basically a no-bullshit guy."

Don Penny saw a basic change in the field of political oratory. "There's no longer any place for rhetoric in the market," he said. "The American people are bored to shit with politicians. They've heard 'Let me be perfectly honest' eighty million times and they don't believe any of it."

Landon Parvin, a WASPish Woodard to Penny's ethnic Bernstein, concurred completely.

Describing the changes in oratory, Parvin said, "It's conversation now, not speeches. We have a U.S. senator who's a client, for example. When he first came to us he was using his hands and flailing around, and we said, 'Why are you doing that?' And he said, 'Well, a speech coach in New York told me I had to use emphasis.' We said, 'Watch Ronald Reagan.' He never moves his hands. He moves his head as he talks. The energy comes from the eyes. Because [movement] detracts from what the person is saying. President Reagan is perfect for television because you can't use large gestures on television."

Penny also gave high marks to the incumbent. "When I started workin' with Ronald Reagan twenty years ago," recalled Penny, "I smelled what was going to happen. And goddammed if it hasn't. I got a company here in Washington that could never had survived ten or even five years ago. But as we speak, the Republicans have twenty-two guys up for the '86 elections. We've got our choice of working with *all* of them or *any* of them!"

Chapter 17
The Modesty Gambit

"I like comedy in Washington. It ain't slick here. It ain't Hollywood. We do Rotarian jokes and the people laugh. You know, home comedy. It ain't Bob Hope."
DON PENNY

A poll of Gerald Ford's friends by *The Washington Post* assembled the following list of adjectives describing the President: "slow, plodding, unimaginative, nonintellectual, poorly staffed, out of touch, pedestrian, inarticulate." The good news was that here was a wealth of material for self-effacing humor. So the Ford image factory set out to create a mythology of modesty for Jerry Ford.

Humor offers a shrewd strategy to any political leader. Since few paragons reach the White House, a leader is likely to have certain frailties that leave him open to attack. Humor is the ideal instrument to defuse them. As Bob Orben expressed it, "You can't fight an attack with reality. You have to fight it with humor."

The public perception of Gerald Ford was of a man over his head, out of control, a caretaker president. And so Ford would kid this perception with lines like this: "I told the Republicans I had a safe seat in Grand Rapids—and look what happened!"

At other times he would bemoan his demanding job: "You

don't need to have a pool at the White House to get in deep water."

Or he would demean the majesty of his position: "I didn't realize how much the honeymoon was over until this morning when the Metro started to build a new station in the Oval Office."

Ford tried to laugh away his dull speaking style with anecdotes like this:

> I was giving a speech once in Omaha and after the speech I was taken to a reception in another part of town. At the reception a sweet old lady came up to me, put her gloved hand in mine and said, "I heard you gave a speech here tonight." And I said, "Oh, it was nothing," and she said, "Yes, that's what I heard."

Jerry Ford made it a point to laugh at all his deficiencies. They were, after all, the flaws of an ordinary man, and Ford judged that the ordinary man would understand them. Said Ford, with disarming candor, "I guess it just proves that in American anyone can be President."

Ford's most serious liability was his reputation for clumsiness. He had fallen down the ramp while emerging from an airliner in Munich, and on another occasion butted his head on the top of a helicopter door.

Bob Orben set out to fight this ridicule with humor and provided the President with some lines like this: "As you can imagine, I don't agree with those who have called me the Evel Knievel of politics." But not everyone in the White House felt that ineptitude could be neutralized with comedy.

"There was a considerable battle over how this criticism should be addressed," Orben told me. "I always wanted to do it with humor. Others thought it would only be calling more attention to it. I lost these battles more often than I won them."

One of Orben's victories was evident in a joke that Ford told on his return from a state visit to China:

When we went to China, at parties and state dinners everybody was always complimenting Betty's dancing. I don't want to sound jealous, but I can dance better than her anytime. I just don't look good in tights.

Ford returned to the theme of his terpsichorean clumsiness when he described the courtship of his wife-to-be:

We would go dancing to the music of big bands. But we had a problem. Betty had studied modern dance and I was a football player. Betty was very polite, never really came right out and said I was a lousy dancer—but she did have an interesting theory as to why I played center rather than quarterback. She said it is one of the few positions where you don't have to move your feet.

There is an irony about the issue of Ford as a stumbler. Chevy Chase to the contrary, Gerald Ford was probably the best-coordinated president in this century. As Orben observed, "We are talking about a fellow who was captain of the Michigan football team, played in the all-star East-West Shrine game, and got offers from two professional football teams." But as most of his predecessors in the White House discovered, it is not easy to fight ridicule with reality.

Orben explained the strategy of humor as the great defuser. When you make light of an issue on which your enemies are attacking, you have said in effect, "Yes, I know the criticism. It's not true. And it's false to the point where I feel comfortable doing jokes about it."

Gerald Ford was a man of immense good humor who never showed his bitterness at the jokes that were being leveled at him, from *Saturday Night Live* and *The Tonight Show*. But he undoubtedly resented them. As Richard Reeves observed, Ford was careful to point out that he had graduated in the top third of his high school class in Grand Rapids. He was rankled by Johnson's slur, which in its sanitized form declared him unable to walk and chew gum simultaneously. Ford began an address to the Yale Law School by saying:

It's a great pleasure to be at the Yale Law School Sesquicentennial Convocation.... And I defy anyone to say that and chew gum at the same time.

Ford was able to defuse some of the clumsiness issue by deprecating his golf game:

What really hurt me was when Arnold Palmer asked if I would not wear his slacks except under an assumed name.... They say you can always tell a good golfer by the number of people in the gallery. You have heard of Arnie's Army. My group is called Ford's Few.... My problem is that I have a wild swing. Back home on my home course they don't yell "Fore," they yell "Ford." ... The Secret Service men you have seen around me today—when I play golf, they qualify for combat pay.... In Washington I am known as the President of the United States, and in golf I am known as the jinx of the links.

Ford made himself the butt of depreciative humor in nearly every sport. It was interesting to note that though he mocked his athletic ability, he was careful to speak at a variety of sporting events, justly emphasizing the fact that he held legitimate credentials in the field of sports.

To an assembly of skiers he declared, "Let's just say I can ski for hours on end." To a yachting association he said, "Is there any correlation between the fact that sailing is one sport that needs a great deal of wind and your invitation for me to speak here tonight?" At Ohio State University he said, "I met Woody Hayes at the airport. We had our picture taken together and when it appears in the *Columbus Dispatch*, I am sure the caption will say: 'Woody Hayes and friend.' "

The most radical effort to defuse the image of Ford as a fumbler and laugh it out of existence was proposed by Don Penny.

Theodore White had described the making of the President. Joe McGinniss had pictured the selling of the President. It remained for Don Penny to propose the clowning of the President.

Despite his desire to neutralize the clumsiness issue with humor, Bob Orben strongly opposed the Penny proposal as unspeakably undignified.

"I was told it was going to create a catastrophe," recalled Penny. "Bob Orben said, 'Oh my God—this is sure not presidential.' He was very concerned, and I said, 'Now Bob, we don't agree here on one basic thing. Now, he's a President, so if you want him to be presidential, then have him fucking sign a treaty! But if you want him to get a laugh, then *listen to me.*'"

The White House was preparing for Ford's appearance at a correspondents' dinner at which the guest of honor would be comedian Chevy Chase. For two years Chase has been ridiculing Jerry Ford's clumsiness on *Saturday Night Live,* showing him walking into doors and falling down stairs. Said Penny, "I told Orben that we'll do a prop gag. And Orben said, 'Oh my God, the President will do a *prop gag?* They'll think it's for real!' I said fine, they'll laugh even more. Humor to me is *alive.* It's like fucking. It's all foreplay."

Penny recalled the prop gag with relish.

"I said to him, 'Mr. President, Chevy Chase has decided to come down to Washington.' I said, 'Before you get up, you're sitting next to him on the dais. So here's what we'll do. We'll put a lot of this heavy railroad silver and pottery in a place that when you get up you will pull this napkin along with you, and you'll pull all this stuff, and dump it right in his lap. Okay? Then you will walk up to the podium. You'll have two speeches, Mr. President. A real speech and a phony one that will be in your hand. You will reach out and let the speech go and fifteen pages will go flying into the audience. And Walter Cronkite and sixty other guys will go racing for the pages—to get you your speech back so you won't fuck up the whole deal.' At which point the President was already laughing and Orben was saying, 'Oh my God . . .' So I said, 'Bob, trust me,' and he said, 'Oh my, the President's going to be sorry,' and I said, 'Bob, I'll bet you everything I got in this world that they're going to eat him up and love him.' At which point Bob said, 'Well, I don't want any part of this.' At which point Jerry Ford looked at him and said, 'Bob, I think you're right. I think you should *not* be involved in this. Let's have Penny take the whole blame.' He smiled at me, and that's when Jerry Ford and Don Penny became real close friends."

At the Chevy Chase dinner the stage was set. The President was introduced. "I was standing there and I saw it happen," said Penny. "The President got up from the table and dropped about sixty pounds of silver all over the floor.... People were screaming.... And he played it beautifully! He said, 'Oh my gosh ... oh shucks ... oh sorry ...' And nobody realized it was set up.... Then he got up there and did the whole speech bit, which worked magnificently! And then he just smiled and he said, 'Good evening, I'm Gerald Ford,' and he turned to Chevy Chase and said, 'And you're not.'

"From then on we were fucking rolling. And Dave Kennerly looked at me with that little rabbit face of his and he said, 'Looks like it's going to work.' And I thought—a kid from Brooklyn, and the President's up there doing the material—and I thought to myself, 'Well, God, You and me did it. Plus a little help from the giant blond gentile.' "

Jerry Ford never quite succeeded in laughing away his image as an amiable bumbler. But he never stopped trying.

In addition to laughing at his clumsiness, his dancing, his golf game, his acumen, and his oratory, he would be forever seeking fresh fields of self-disparagement.

President Ford reached the zenith of self-mockery in laughing at his own backside. One of his favorite jokes recalled how he was introduced by a former teammate at the University of Michigan. Said Ford:

He introduced me by saying, "Ladies and gentlemen, I played football with Jerry Ford and it made a lasting impression on me. I was a quarterback and Jerry was the center. And you might say it gave me a completely different view of the President of the United States.

In addition to kidding his own posterior, Ford was not above mocking his spreading middle. Addressing the Reserve Officers Association, he said:

> Before coming here tonight I started reminiscing about my active service some years ago. I was telling my wife how our ship won the war in the Pacific. I got a little nostalgic and then I made a tactical error. I tried to put on my old Navy uniform. Have you noticed how something happens to those old uniforms when you keep them in the closet too long? They start to shrink, particularly around the middle.

Ford was a simple man and he got political mileage out of fostering that image. Early in his term, a photo of Ford toasting his own English muffins, while his wife slept off camera, won wide circulation. Ford wasted no time in exploiting this image of conjugal sensitivity. Speaking on sexual discrimination, he said:

> I think you all know where I stand on this issue. As I prove every morning at breakfast time, I certainly don't believe that a woman's place is in the kitchen.

Jerry Ford had no taste for blue stories. As Bob Hartmann told me, "He didn't like dirty jokes. You told him a dirty joke at your peril. He would give you no reaction. He pretended he didn't understand—and maybe he didn't." Yet on occasion, like a gagwriter trying to slip a salacious joke past a network censor, Orben would insert a line like this in the presidential repertoire:

> You know, people say a lot of nice things about Vice Presidents. But it is almost like being the best man at a wedding— you never get a chance to prove it.

It is an unexplained paradox that despite Ford's distaste for bawdy humor, he enjoyed joking about his eye for the ladies. On one occasion he told a University of Michigan audience:

> In my freshman year I had a job at the University Hospital. I was a very disinterested waiter in the interns' dining room and a very energetic waiter in the nurses' cafeteria. I worked in the interns' dining room for their benefit and the nurses' dining room for my benefit.

Ford seemed to be preoccupied with the fair sex and basked in the sudden attention that his instant presidency brought him.

One evening, Vikki Carr, a pretty songstress of Mexican descent, entertained at a White House dinner. When she asked the President his favorite Mexican dish, he replied, "You are."

Milton Friedman, a talented and witty Ford speechwriter, told me a story that exemplified Ford's roving eye. Said Friedman, "In Indianapolis Bob Orben and I were writing the President's speech. There was a reception before dinner. There was a group of gorgeous young women from the Young Republicans group. Ford was really enjoying their attention—they were clustering around him. We pulled him away for some final work on the speech and took him into a side room. He stared at us and said, 'With all the gorgeous girls here—I end up looking at Friedman and Orben!' "

The pedestal of modesty that Ford's imagists built for him was occasionally undermined by some decidedly nasty cracks.

Esquire magazine conferred a Dubious Achievement Award for bitchiness on Ford for his comment about Ronald Reagan:

> There is a lot of silly speculation on whether Ronnie dyes his hair. Which is ridiculous. Governor Reagan does *not* dye his hair. Let's say he's turning prematurely orange.

On another occasion, in admiring decorations at a banquet, Ford said:

I love that wall of roses. Wouldn't that make a great corsage for Bella Abzug? . . . No, I'm only kidding. I have a great admiration for Bella Abzug. In fact, we both use the same slogan: "I am my own man."

Of George Wallace he said, "Now there's a horse of a different color. In your heart, you know he's white."

Of Harold Stassen he said, "Let's not forget Harold Stassen—wouldn't it be great if we could?"

Of President Johnson he said, "Henry Clay always said he'd rather be right than president. Now President Johnson has proved it really is a choice."

Of Robert Kennedy he said, "Bobby's now at that awkward age. He's too young to be president and he's too old for that haircut."

Of Jimmy Carter he said, "Let me congratulate Governor Carter on his fine speech. That's the Governor over there. It's easy to see where he sits. Now if we could only figure out where he stands."

Speaking in Los Angeles, Ford committed the astonishing feat of insulting both the UCLA and USC football teams in one slighting gibe. He said:

It is a pleasure to be in California again. California—the state that puts together such great football teams as the UCLA Bruins and the USC Trojans. As a former football player for the Big Ten, I have always been grateful for those practice teams you have given us to play against. Well, we call it practice—I think you call it the Rose Bowl.

In spinning jokes out of his own frailties, Jerry Ford was careful to omit the telling detail that might really diminish him in the eyes of his audience. He often told the story of how Richard Nixon had phoned him with the good news that he was to be the new Vice-President. The story described a farcical scene in which Jerry asked the President to hang up and call back on another line so Betty could listen on an extension.

132

It painted a picture of Ford as innocent and amiable, and one could laugh along with his embarrassment. But what Ford did *not* say in the anecdote was that Nixon had had such contempt for Ford that he could not bring himself to make the call, and had Alexander Haig do it for him. In the fun-filled anecdote, Alexander Haig was dropped from the story.

Part Four
RICHARD M. NIXON

"The President, with the enormous responsibility
that he has, must not be constantly preening in
front of a mirror. . . . I don't worry about polls. I
don't worry about image. . . . I never have."
RICHARD M. NIXON

Chapter 18
The Last Laugh

"Into this [television] milieu came Richard
Nixon: grumpy, cold, and aloof. . . . [He was
not] one of the boys."
                              JOE McGINNISS,
                         The Selling of the President

I met Joe McGinniss on the train that carried Bobby Kennedy's body to Arlington Cemetery. He was a bright young columnist for the *Philadelphia Inquirer* who was writing a magazine article on Richard Nixon's image-making efforts on television. That article would expand into a bestselling, groundbreaking book on image making in American politics called *The Selling of the President*.

Joe McGinniss pointed out that politics and television are part of a con game in which voters are sold the illusion of omniscient presidents. The voter, said Joe, clings to the delusion that his president is wise and wonderful, and television helps promote the illusion.

McGinniss related, in riveting detail, how the candidate and his TV advisers painted a picture of wisdom and warmth for Richard Nixon in his victorious campaign for the presidency.

If politics and advertising are both con games in which we are sold tainted products—from politicians to fast food—the same may be said of comedy. The stand-up comedian sells us the tainted proposition that life is a barrel of laughs and that all our troubles are transitory. Comedy provides the escape from reality that movies did during the Depression.

But comedy was a part of the con game that Richard Nixon was ill equipped to employ. He could never handle humor in the effortless way of a Jack Kennedy or a Ronald Reagan.

Humor is the sleight of hand that enables our presidents to escape a hanging for their mistakes. But Richard Nixon was never able to use it to soften up the public. Where Jack Kennedy had had an ironic, understated wit that made us blind to his flaws, Nixon was intense, harsh, sanctimonious. Though he opened doors to Red China, though he functioned brilliantly in foreign affairs, when he was trapped in the morass of Watergate there was not an ounce of tolerance in the public or press.

Unfortunately for Richard Nixon, humor cannot be taught. If it were teachable, Richard Nixon would have learned it. Bob Orben or Don Penny or one of the elite corps of capital court jesters could have come in once a week to make Nixon funny. Alas, this was not possible.

Joseph Heller, whose irreverent, biting humor drove the greatest comic novel of our time, *Catch-22*, has said that something in one's personality makes one funny. But it is not a transferable talent, said Heller. "An appreciation of humor and the ability to create it cannot be taught. Either they are in a person's character or they are not."

From Nixon's point of view, it was not really desirable that his wit should sparkle. He would sometimes say, "The public doesn't have to like me. But they'll respect me." The public wasn't so sure. E. B. White observed that whatever else an American believes about himself, "he is absolutely sure he has a sense of humor." White might have added that an American also feels that every decent man *should* have a sense of humor.

But humor was not a part of Richard Nixon's personality and this proved a fatal flaw. The determined exploitation of humor by politicians from Adlai Stevenson to John F. Kennedy was apparent to the analytical mind of Richard Nixon. But recognizing a need is not the same as fulfilling it. As Joe Heller observed, "Many people go through life without ever cracking a smile or making a joke." Nixon badly needed humor but lacked the personality to capture it. That was his Catch-22.

Humor does not make the frontal assault of oratory; it is more insidious. While one is laughing, one's guard is down, and the adroit politician can slip in his message with the laughter, as Bernard Shaw did in his plays. Nixon was the Ibsen of presidents.

Advertisers have learned to sell with humor—as in the commercials for Miller Lite in which various luminaries quarrel over whether the product tastes great or is less filling. As we laugh, they are selling us beer. As we laugh at politicians, they are selling themselves and their ideologies.

Since presidential elections have become popularity contests that are decided mainly on catch phrases and punchlines, it is inevitable that the presidents we elect by this whimsical process will not be exceptional.

Speculations on how President A would have ruled if he'd had the qualities of President B are provocative. For example, if Richard Nixon had had Ronald Reagan's geniality and his ability to make friends, Nixon's presidency might not have ended in disgrace. Character is fate, and Nixon's flaws led inexorably to his doom.

The flaw, some will say, is not in ourselves but in our system. No other democracy chooses its leaders the way America does. Says *The New Republic*'s irrepressible TRB, "The way we [elect our president] always fascinates me and awes me, yes, and frightens me a little. Someday, I think, it is going to get us into trouble."

In his classic volume *The American Commonwealth*, Britain's

U.S. ambassador Lord Bryse asks the question "Why is this great office [of president] not more frequently filled by great men?" Bryse's answer is distressing—and right on the money. He says we always choose the *safe* candidate, not the brilliant one. He says the American voter wants his president to be likable, sensible, and magnetic. No device is more supportive of such an impression than humor.

TRB acknowledges that a president may be brilliant and still manage to win election, but only if he is careful to conceal his brilliance. It is like Joyce Brothers's advice to intelligent women on dates: When he makes the wrong turn off the freeway, don't tell him. It is the same in business. In corporate politics it is essential to be ambitious and fatal to appear so. In electoral politics it is useful to be brilliant but fatal to appear so.

Richard Nixon's speeches and press conferences needed the leavening of humor that he was never able to give them. Bob Markel, the astute former editor of Grosset and Dunlap, worked closely with the former President on his memoir, *R.N.* Markel told me of his visits to Nixon at San Clemente and their frequent conversations. Markel is a charming, witty man who invites cordiality. He related many things Nixon said— some solemn, some thoughtful, some instructive—but never a word of wit.

Said Orben, a sense of humor "is one of the attributes a [politician] must have. The goodwill engendered by humor goes a long way in covering his gaffes."

Richard Nixon has been accused by his detractors of being too manipulative by half. It may be said in his favor that unlike others who have occupied the Oval Office, he has never used the manipulations of humor.

Were it not for humor's ability to distort and deceive, one could find little wrong with a sense of humor in a U.S. president. As Joseph Heller observed, "A person who has the ability to laugh will be more tolerant. . . . Humor can be very instrumental in helping to keep things in perspective."

The importance of Nixon's lack of humor is viewed best in the light of a comment by Richard Drayne of CBS News, who often feeds jokes to Teddy Kennedy. Said Drayne, "Presidents without a sense of humor make me nervous."

Chapter 19
You Think
That's Funny?

"Nixon was insecure and lacking in self-confidence, so it was very difficult for him to make
fun of himself."
HUGH SIDEY

If humor is a reflection of self-confidence, and its absence an
indication of lack of personal security, Richard Nixon's
dearth of humor quite clearly says something about the flaws
of his character.

Bill Adler, the protean anthologist who has published a series of books delineating the wit of our recent presidents—beginning with *The Kennedy Wit*, followed by *The Johnson Humor*,
The Ford Wit, and *The Wit and Wisdom of Jimmy Carter*—was
defied by the absence of quotable humor from the lips of
Richard Nixon. An examination of Adler's book *The Washington Wits*, which embraces the humorous utterances of political
figures from Hubert Humphrey to Everett Dirksen, offers a
scant six jokes attributed to Nixon in his thirty years of public
life—and most of them are decidedly anemic.

Most presidents are not the authors of many of their witty
utterances, but a good deal of their humor is genuinely spontaneous. Often the circumstances are such that they could not
have been ghostwritten. But Richard Nixon seems to have

been incapable, by inclination or ability, of expressing himself with humor.

Of course, once the genie of Watergate was out of the bottle few would have expected to find Nixon a font of wit, except perhaps a certain gallows humor. But even during his first term as president, his eight years with Eisenhower, and his years in House and Senate, the product of his wit could fit nicely on a postcard.

Calls to Nixon speechwriters, including Bill Safire, David Gergen, Ben Stein, and others, inquiring after examples of the Nixon wit went unanswered, perhaps to spare me fruitless conversation. The scribes of our other presidents were more forthcoming.

Hugh Sidey, *Time*'s perspicacious White House columnist, has observed seven presidents and attributed Nixon's mirthlessness to the fact that "his Quaker parents didn't raise their children to take the world lightly." Added Sidey, "Nixon did have a wry look at other world leaders. But he was insecure and so lacking in self-confidence that it was very difficult for him to chide himself." Self-disparaging humor was beyond Richard Nixon.

Bob Orben said that he simply could not help a Richard Nixon to be humorous. "You could only help a president if he wanted to be humorized," said Orben. Richard Nixon did not.

Orben recalled an analogous situation with a high-ranking corporate executive. "I was brought in to lighten him up," said Orben. "When I was brought in and introduced to him, it was apparent to me that he wanted no part of me. And I labored with trying to brighten his speeches and trying to add humor. And it finally became apparent that it wasn't going to work. He wouldn't rehearse, he wouldn't do the material; the one or two times he did try it, without rehearsal, it came across like the reading of the will. Finally I quit. It was only later that I realized that this man had been brought up in a very strict, Calvinist household and believed that we are not put on this earth to enjoy life. . . . The last thing his emotions would let him do was to stand up and tell jokes in front of an audience." Like Orben's austere executive, Richard Nixon was raised in a strict household where piety was more highly prized than levity.

Aram Bakshian, onetime speech and humor writer for Ronald Reagan, had also written for Richard Nixon. He was the sole Nixon speechwriter willing to discuss the Nixonian persona, and he painted his patron as aloof and humorless, lacking the warmth and wit of a Ronald Reagan. "The contrast between Nixon and Reagan was marked," said Bakshian. "With Nixon it was sometimes interesting to write for him. But he wasn't the sort of person you'd get chummy with. Most politicians who've gotten to the top are driven people. . . ." Nixon was driven in a way that Ronald Reagan is not, and it showed in the absence of Nixon's humor and the abundance of Reagan's.

Nixon in college must have had a gaiety and wit that evaporated in the harsh climate of public life. Pat Nixon recalled a very different Richard Nixon on the Whittier College campus: "Our group used to get together often. . . . We would sit around and tell stories and laugh. Dick was always the highlight of the party because he had a wonderful sense of humor. He would keep everybody in stitches. . . . We used to put on funny shows. It was all good, clean fun, and we had loads of laughs."

But despite his lack of humor and his other flaws of personality, Richard Nixon survived. He survived, some said, because he was shrewd and resilient and could cut corners when the need arose. He failed against Jack Kennedy in 1960 because he lacked some of the qualities that were mandatory in a candidate at the start of the television age. He hadn't the foggiest notion of how to use TV to seduce an impressionable public. Television would prove a quagmire for a harsh, determined, humorless man like Nixon and a triumph for the handsome, cocky, witty image of a Jack Kennedy—or a Ronald Reagan. The camera can be cruel, and it revealed in stark candor Nixon's naked appetite for office.

But Richard Nixon would not make the same mistake twice. When Nixon ran for the presidency again in '68, he hired an advertising expert named Harry Treleaven to correct his visible flaws. One of these was Nixon's lack of humor. Wrote Treleaven in a strategy memo retrieved for posterity by Joe McGinniss:

> HUMOR—Can be corrected to a degree, but let's not be too obvious about it. Romney's cornball attempts have hurt him. If we're going to be witty, let a pro write the words.

Where a Ronald Reagan would idly spin off dozens of anecdotes to promote his views, Nixon's use of anecdotes was often simply historical, like the Nixon tapes. In planning for ceremonies at the White House, he ordered that his aides nominate a number of "anecdotists" to go to every White House event at which something of humorous interest might occur. He wanted them recorded for the President's file—for history. He was not hungry for humor, but he knew history's appetite for anecdotes and, in his own obsessive way, was making sure they would be captured for the future.

Nixon did not welcome spontaneous humor in his aides and agency heads. Toward the end of a crisis involving the postal service, somebody suggested to the President that the postal unions might not be committed to the support of his postal reforms. An aide tried to make a joke of the matter, and Nixon rasped with chilling intensity, "Let's stop this horsing around!" The abrupt and abrasive reaction was typical of Nixon's response to levity in serious situations.

As Gerald Ford was tone deaf to oratory, Richard Nixon was tone deaf to humor. Though he had some extremely witty men on his staff—Paul Keyes, the chief comedy writer for Jack Paar and for NBC's *Laugh-In*, and the witty and articulate William Safire—Nixon made scant use of their comedic talents.

Unlike Kennedy, Johnson, Ford, Carter, and Reagan, Richard Nixon employed no writers whose time was devoted—in full or in part—to the creation of comedy. Nixon's advocates will applaud this as the mark of a serious man with no time for triviality. His critics, who are somewhat more numerous, will see it as a sign of rigidity and neurosis. Psychologists will find in this indifference to humor a blindness to the absurdities of life and the ironies of fate.

In any case, it was a deficiency that robbed Nixon of much of the joy of life. Pat Nixon attended a Republican fundraiser in Chicago where in his address the President warned Republicans against "the temptation to stand pat on what we have done." One reporter who covered the dinner was aghast at the headline his city desk put on the top of the story: CAN'T STAND PAT, SAYS NIXON. Where another president might have chuckled at the headline and drawn laughter from subsequent audiences, Nixon grimly altered his wording. Next time he delivered the speech, he said Republicans must resist "the temptation to stand still. . . ."

John Osborne, the brilliant correspondent who covered the Nixon White House for *The New Republic*, has testified to Nixon's lack of humor at every press conference. As he approached the dais, recalled Osborne, Nixon's every move, his every detail of dress, expression, and demeanor spoke of what a later generation would characterize as "uptight." It was not a mode that lent itself to humor, which requires an untrammeled spirit. "The restless hands, the seemingly unmanageable fingers, the twitching mouth, the frozen smile that would appear for an instant and then vanish," all these testified, said Osborne, to the sober, solemn man beneath.

If humor is a sign of perspective in a president, then this was a man trapped in the narrow corridors of thought and anxiety. Small wonder that Richard Nixon remained invisible to much of the press much of the time, screened by a phalanx of aides. The men who shielded him from public view must have felt that disclosure would not be in the incumbent's best interests. Humor would be a window opened to press and public and this president preferred to be shielded from eye and understanding.

Nixon was sometimes guilty of unintentional humor. Broadcaster Ted Koppel tells of returning to his home on Long Island from ABC's Manhattan studio where he broadcasts his *Nightline* show. Koppel had arrived home late after an interview with Nixon and fallen asleep at about four A.M. At eight the phone jangled him awake and he picked up the receiver.

"Hello?" said Koppel groggily.

"This is Richard Nixon," said the unmistakable voice at the other end.

"What can I do for you, Mr. President?" asked Koppel.

Nixon paused a moment.

"I didn't realize you got up this early," he said.

In January of 1961 the six million readers of *Time* magazine were surprised and amused to read a sample of unaccustomed Nixonian wit. One of *Time*'s readers was less amused but equally surprised since he knew that the humor was his own and had been inadvertently attributed to Nixon. It was the week of John F. Kennedy's epochal inaugural address and Ted Sorensen had spoken before the Washington press corps at an off-the-record luncheon. Here is how Sorensen recalled it later:

> I began, totally fictitiously of course, saying that I had been in California the previous week and had run into Richard Nixon, and that Nixon had said to me, "I watched the Kennedy Inaugural and I have to admit that there were words he said that I wish *I* had said." And I said to him, "Well, thank you, Mr. Vice-President. You mean the part about 'Ask not what your country can do for you'? And he said, "No, I mean the part about, 'I do solemnly swear...'"

Sorensen had invented the exchange with Nixon, but *Time*'s correspondent in the audience had accepted Sorensen's droll version of the conversation as factual. "So the following week," said Sorensen, "*Time* magazine had an article on Nixon that said among other things: 'The former Vice-President has not lost his sense of humor....' " Indeed he hadn't. If the story had been true it would have been more accurate to say he had found it.

"Nixon had no sense of humor at all," reflected Sorensen. "I just think it was his set of mind. I think he was a very intelligent man but he took himself extremely seriously, and there was a certain bitterness about his approach to life and people that didn't allow for much sense of humor."

Ronald Reagan's background as an actor equipped him to be a splendid performer on the stage of public life. It enabled him to bring both drama and humor to the presidency and to enjoy the fruits of immense popular approval. Yet Richard Nixon also had a background in acting, and it did little to help him win an audience.

Nixon's career as an actor blossomed at Whittier College, where he wrote his fraternity's first play. It was called *The Trysting Place*, and young Dick Nixon was both its director and its male lead. Nixon's detractors have often observed that there is something of the actor in many of his public appearances. On seeing Nixon weeping after his famous Checkers speech, his drama professor at Whittier boasted, "I taught him how to cry."

Nixon's delivery of the Checkers speech produced another notable plaudit. He recalled a phone call from the president of Twentieth Century-Fox, moviemaker Darryl F. Zanuck, who had declared, "The most tremendous performance I've ever seen!" This was damning with exuberant praise. Though Richard Nixon was preoccupied with acting, the flaws in his nature prevented him from excelling in its lighter vein, an area in which Kennedy and Reagan sparkled. Had he developed a sense of humor and perspective, it might have spared him much of the tragedy of his public life and let him enjoy more of its triumphs.

One observer of the Watergate scandal speculated that had Nixon been able to see his own flaws—which is the essence of humor—he might have displayed either contrition or irony at the excesses of his administration. We have all seen humor defuse sins as great and sinners as venal. But never was there a more humorless pack of miscreants than those who "stonewalled" the charges of malefaction. Since Nixon was incapable of seeing himself through the self-mocking eyes of humor, his lack of wit combined with his paranoia to undo him.

Eleanor Roosevelt once observed, "We grow up when we have our first good laugh—at ourselves." The quality that has set our best presidents apart from the rest—from Lincoln to Kennedy to Reagan—has been their willingness not to take themselves too seriously.

Humor is most objectionable when it is used to deceive and dissemble, not when it lights the reflective mind and adds perspective and insight. Nixon, unlike Lincoln, Kennedy, and Reagan, seemed to take himself far too seriously for his own good, and lacked the basic sense of security that would have let him laugh at himself.

If Norman Cousins demonstrated the therapeutic effects of humor in curing disease, Richard Nixon demonstrated the malign effects of its lack, if not to one's physical health, at least to one's political survival.

In his penetrating work *In Search of Nixon: A Psychohistorical Inquiry*, Bruce Mazlish observes that Nixon seemed compelled to think well of himself, to feel he was just and noble. It is said we judge others by their actions and ourselves by our motives. Nixon was his own best defense attorney, unwilling to concede any faults or flaws. He would have been well served by an ability to acknowledge his own warts and laugh at them. But there was no ironic self-examination for Richard Nixon.

There was none of the self-disparagement of which the witty man is capable. Adlai Stevenson, for example, could mock himself, recalling the time he encountered a woman at the Democratic National Convention. "She was eight months pregnant," said Adlai, "and she was carrying a sign that said, 'STEVENSON'S THE MAN.' "

Remembering Nixon's speeches and press conferences, says Mazlish, one recalls a man insulated by self-righteousness, a man beleaguered by foes in the press, the public, and the Congress. A man who denied to the world, and to himself, any unworthy instincts. One of the chief virtues of humor is that it grants us the grace to acknowledge our own lack of saintliness and laugh at our own deficiencies. Nixon was denied this assuaging effect.

One reads the hundreds of thousands of words spoken or written by Richard Nixon in a variety of public forums over a third of a century of public service and seeks in vain for a trace of self-deprecating humor, or indeed humor of any kind. It is a saddening search, for what it reveals as well as for what is undiscovered.

Nixon proved in the late sixties what Jimmy Carter proved in the late seventies—that the self-righteous man is often an uncritical man. Nixon saw himself as a man of justice and principle who was being smeared and savaged by his enemies. Most people in public life feel unfairly abused at times, but most are willing to face the flaws in their nature, and humor lets them live with their blemishes. Nixon came to grief in large part because he was never able to look at himself and laugh.

Chapter 20
The Regular Fellow

"Good morning, David. Did you do any fornicating this weekend?"
RICHARD M. NIXON
[to David Frost]

Ben Stein, the witty, acerbic former speechwriter for Richard Nixon, is now a columnist and novelist in Los Angeles. Speaking to his agent about the subject of my book, I said, "I'd like to get Ben's recollections of the Nixon humor."

"What humor?" she asked.

Most of us recall little humor flowing from the Nixon years. If one were to list the ten qualities most closely associated with Richard M. Nixon, humor would fail to make the list. Extend the list to fifty and humor still fails to find a home.

They say that inside every fat man is a thin man trying to get out. It may be that within each humorless man is a witty one trying to emerge. This unlikely thesis is suggested by a story related by Theodore Sorensen.

"Let me tell you a story about Nixon," said Sorensen. "In 1961 I was out in California to give a talk and Nixon was at the same luncheon, and actually he demonstrated a good sense of humor. This was the Ten Outstanding Young Men of the Year Award, given by the National Jaycees. And several of us were standing around outside the luncheon where Nixon was the speaker. And a little gnarled old waiter came up to him and said, 'Hello, Dick, how are ya? How's Pat?' And they had a little chat, very friendly. And then the little old guy limped away in his tattered busboy outfit. And we all looked a little astonished at Nixon and he looked at us and said in a very low, calm voice, with perfect timing: 'That was one of *last* year's ten outstanding young men.' "

If presidents pay an excessive amount of attention to image—and humor is a chief ingredient of image—it is because the lesson of history is clear on its importance to the voter.

No president better appreciated the value of image than Richard Nixon. He was defeated by an unknown young senator named John F. Kennedy, and many suspect that the Kennedy charisma explained his razor-thin victory. It probably happened in the TV debates when the cameras turned their cruel lenses on the sweating Nixon, wetting his lips while Kennedy spoke, and then on the buoyant Kennedy, frankly laughing as Nixon lectured him on morality and Cuba. Kennedy's laughter profoundly altered Nixon's future. Laughter was a more potent weapon than is dreamed of in Norman Cousins' philosophy. Kennedy's laughter and Nixon's sweat swung an election to the lanky Irishman.

No one could claim with justice that this was a sensible way to choose a president. No election should be settled by an unattended trickle forming on a man's chin. In the age of television, what chance would the ugly Abe Lincoln have? He would pose a formidable problem for his imagists.

So Nixon lost the television test and the election, and it taught him a painful lesson. He studied it carefully the next time he reached for the brass ring. It taught him the value of image, and to the cold, intense Nixon it taught the value of laughter.

Humor did not come easily to Richard Nixon. Observing him at close range at a White House press conference, correspondent John Osborne saw a man apparently at ease in a well-cut, wrinkleless suit. Osborne observed the tanned, gently smiling face, a president ostensibly at ease. Yet when the questions ended, Osborne saw a man who was tense and tired. The performance that had seemed so relaxed and friendly was for Richard Nixon a draining deception.

If ever there was a president who would have profited from humor it was Richard Nixon. Johnson was able to use it to mask his anger; Ford used it to exploit his modesty; Carter used it to soften his self-righteousness. But Nixon needed it as a drowning man needs a life raft. During his days in the Oval Office there was the uneasy perception that a great many people out there, "the people we fly over," as Jim Aubrey used to call them, really didn't like Richard Nixon. This fear dominated, darkened, and ultimately demolished the Nixon White House. The President perceived this unstated public antipathy. He once acknowledged to an intimate that he didn't expect to be adored by the public. George McGovern, his opponent in '72, said, "I don't think the country likes that guy." Nixon perceived, intellectually at least, the power of humor to temper his presidential persona. And so, despite his disinclination to play the clown, despite his awkwardness with humorous lines, despite his lack of timing and tempo, he made an effort to incorporate humor into his speeches.

Nixon could recognize the value of humor but he had trouble making it work for him. He once quoted James Thurber as saying that "the oldest and most precious national asset of a country is humor," but for Nixon this was much like declaring the value of truth as an excuse for parting with little of it.

Nixon's humor would always tend to be sparse, tentative, and forced. When he was undergoing a series of interviews by David Frost, he sought a regular-fellow attitude and failed signally. One Monday morning, when he resumed the taped interviews that had begun the previous week, Nixon greeted Frost by saying, "Good morning, David. Did you do any fornicating this weekend?"

Addressing his White House staff he tried for an avuncular manner, seemingly winking at staff adultery:

> This is hard work [in the White House]. It is work that certainly takes you away from your families a great deal. I know some of your wives call me from time to time just to be sure. But I always tell them the right thing.

Addressing a business group in the East Room, Nixon returned to the humor of philandering when he said:

> We have cuff links and a pin for all of you here tonight, for those who are here with your wives. And for those whose wives could not come, we will give you one of these to take home to prove where you were.

Comparisons are always odious, but a comparison of Nixon's remarks to those of Kennedy's on the same occasion shows the low level of wit of the former. Speaking at West Point to issue the traditional proclamation of amnesty, Nixon said:

> My military aide . . . came up and nudged me just a few minutes ago. He said, "You forgot, sir." I said, "What did I forget?" "You forgot something in your speech. You forgot the most important thing." I began to ask him what it was, and he just handed it to me. So I would like to ask if you would have the Adjutant read this to the Corps. I don't know how this is done.

Whereupon the brigade adjutant read a proclamation of amnesty for cadets who were undergoing punishment for infractions of military regulations.

Given the same circumstances, here is how President Kennedy carried out the task of granting amnesty. He said:

> I would like to announce at this time that as Commander-in-Chief I am exercising my privilege of directing the Secretary of the Army and the Superintendent of West Point to remit all

existing confinements and other cadet punishments.... My own confinement goes for another two and a half years, and I may ask it to be extended instead of remitted.

During the presidential campaign, Kennedy often one-upped Nixon, turning Nixon's stern demeanor back on him with laughter. Said Kennedy:

I have seen pictures of Mr. Khrushchev with Mr. Nixon's finger under his nose. Friday night, after the debate, when I went over to shake hands with Mr. Nixon, and the photographers came, suddenly the finger came up in my nose. I thought here it comes, he is going to tell me how wrong I am about the plight of America. And do you know what he said? "Senator, I hear you have been getting better crowds than I have in Cleveland."

Nixon struggled to be as funny as he could. Addressing the graduation exercise at the FBI Academy, he thanked his hosts for the cuff links he was given bearing the FBI crest. Said President Nixon:

I am honored to have these cuff links and I will be honored to wear them. As some of you may know, when I travel through the country, like all presidents, there are times when over-enthusiastic people will grab your arm and take a cuff link. When I wear these I will simply say, "Watch out, the FBI will get them back."

There was a heavy-handedness to Nixon's jokes and a built-in reminder that the speaker was the President of the United States. Comedian Rich Little was on target when he gently ridiculed Nixon in his comedy album *I Am the President*, for it was much a part of the Nixon persona to remind the listener, and perhaps himself, that he was the President, and thus entitled to attention and respect. So where other presidents used humor to break down the barrier of awe between power and the public, Nixon used humor to maintain it.

155

Nixon sought humor on a visit to Idaho, and undermined it with a reminder of his exalted position. He said:

This is the first visit I have made to Idaho since being President of the United States, and I am proud that I am in Idaho Falls. The time was October in the year 1954, and all of these young people here were not even born yet. I remember it was snowing, very heavy snow. Does it still snow here in October?

Another example of the Nixon wit, wedded to the Nixon pomposity, could be observed in his remarks at the annual convention of the Associated Milk Producers. Said Nixon:

I have probably addressed more conventions than any American political figure. I have probably addressed more audiences in America and in the world than any American political figure. This is the biggest convention and the biggest indoor crowd I have ever seen in my life, and I am proud to be here. With 40,000 in this hall, I just wonder who is home milking the cows.

Nixon made an effort at humility when he addressed a dinner honoring Mamie Eisenhower at which a number of Hollywood and Broadway stars were present. Said Nixon:

To those who have participated in the program, they are all here on the stage, but let me say that I came with Mrs. Nixon farther than anybody else, 5,000 miles. I just love to come and see some celebrities.

The "regular fellow" syndrome was again in evidence at a White House dinner when President Nixon embraced Sammy Davis, Jr., and exclaimed:

First, I asked Sammy Davis to come over for a reason. He has probably forgotten this, but I will always remember it. Seventeen years ago, on one of the few evenings when I was vicepresident when we had a little time off in New York, we went over to the Copacabana Restaurant. He was performing. He was a young star. And he performed, I remember, with his father and his uncle. And I said to them, "This has to be the very best that possibly could be done in the field of entertainment." And Sammy said, "Well, you're probably right."

Sammy Davis seemed to bring out the antic mood in Richard Nixon. A few months later, at a Youth rally, Nixon embraced Davis again and found humor in their humble beginnings. Said Nixon:

When Sammy and I were chatting, I want you to know it was one of the most moving experiences for me and I hope it was for him. We talked about our backgrounds. We both came from rather poor families. . . . We both have done rather well.

Nixon's failure in the 1960 presidential campaign made him understandably bitter. To his credit he was able to laugh at his failure when he said of himself that he was "a dropout from the Electoral College, because I flunked debating."

Nixon employed humor to present himself as the traditional family man, which meant making his wife the subject of many of his lines. When a crowd at the GOP convention in Miami began chanting, "We want Pat!" Nixon responded, "You can't have her. I've got to keep her."

Nixon's detractors would find his frequent invocations of his wife's name cloying. Nixon said after the convention in Miami:

Mr. President and Pat—because she is the First Lady of the land, but I think in the hearts of all of us she is "Pat," and we are just going to take advantage of it and keep it that way. . . . And those people who tried to pretend that what was taking place the last few days in Miami Beach was unexciting because we knew how it was going to turn out. Well, I have never seen a John Wayne movie that was unexciting because you knew he was going to get the bad guy in the end.

Nixon went for double casino when he invoked the names of both his wife and his mother, in addressing a women's group:

> When I think back, I remember especially the influence of my mother. My mother had perhaps more influence on me than my father. I think it rather works that way. The mother often influences the boy, and the father may influence the daughter more. I am not sure Mrs. Nixon agrees with me with regard to our daughter. . . .

In a speech at San Diego Airport, Nixon concluded by thanking entertainer Art Linkletter, who was campaigning with him. Said Nixon, in an atypical attempt at ribald humor:

> When Art Linkletter talks about all that business of breakfast and dinner with Pat, I just want to keep the record straight. He has slept in the White House. He slept in the Queen's Room. When Pat's room is being painted, she sleeps there, so we can say that Art Linkletter has slept in Pat's bed.

Richard Nixon liked to dismiss the whole notion of image as beneath his notice. "People are much less interested in image," said Nixon, "than are columnists." This view of the voter as indifferent to matters of image did not square with the cautionary memo that a Nixon adviser sent him during the '68 campaign, declaring, "Voters are basically lazy, basically uninterested in making an effort to understand what we're talking about. . . . It takes effort to follow a logical argument."

In other words, it is a struggle to follow specific issues, while it is easier to form a judgment based on image.

With Nixon as with other presidential candidates, there was often a sizable disparity between the image and the fact. This was especially true in the area of profanity. Nixon presented himself as a pious man who would never employ blasphemy in his speech. He denounced former president Truman for his use of expletives and declared that America's youth should have a president who, like himself, never resorted to earthy language. When a White House correspondent reported on Nixon's use of the copulative verb—the precise quotation was "Fuck the ABA!"—presidential aide John Erlichman wrote to the publication and said:

> Sirs:
> I noted your reference to a profane remark attributed to the President. The President's use of this obscenity in describing the ABA was supposed to have taken place during a meeting in the President's office during the morning of Friday, October 2. I happened to be present for that entire meeting. I would like to set the record straight. The President did not use the quoted obscenity at any time during that meeting. The simple fact is that in the many hours I have spent with the President I have never heard him use the word attributed to him. . . .

When the White House transcripts were released in the heat of the Watergate scandal and the public saw the thicket of "expletives deleted," which given their context left little doubt of what verbs, nouns, and modifiers had been used, it was apparent that the Nixon piety was so much sanctimony. By then, Ehrlichman's credibility was also open to serious doubt.

Long before, Nixon's proclaimed distaste for profanity had been the subject of a telling bit of humor by Jack Kennedy at a dinner honoring Al Smith. JFK tucked his tongue firmly in cheek and said:

> One of the inspiring notes that was struck in the last debate was struck by the Vice-President in his very moving warning to the children of the nation and the candidates against the use of profanity in presidents. But I am told that a prominent Republican said to him yesterday in Jacksonville, Fla., "Mr. Nixon, that was a damn fine speech." And the Vice-President said, "I appreciate the compliment but not the language." And

the Republican went on, "Yes sir, I liked it so much that I contributed a thousand dollars to your campaign." And Mr. Nixon said, "The hell you say."

No area of national life better suggests the "regular fellow" than the field of sports. And so Richard Nixon tried manfully to mine humor from his interest in the sporting life.

At a Republican victory dinner in May 1969, he embraced "the national pastime," saying:

I am a baseball fan, and you prove it by being for the [Washington] Senators, believe me. I was reminded of the fact that they may be doing better primarily because they have a new manager. And I was also reminded of the fact before I came in here that the new manager almost didn't make it. Everett Dirksen was going to stop him in the Senate. When Ev heard that some fellow by the name of Ted was going to take over his Senators, his hair stood on end. [Nixon's pun referred to Ted Williams, manager of the Washington Senators, and Ted Kennedy, the new Senate whip.]

Nixon again turned to the baseball diamond with a story he told during his 1960 presidential campaign:

When Yogi Berra went to the World Series to play the first game between the Braves and the Yankees, one of the wives of the Braves wanted to meet the very colorful catcher of the Yankees. Yogi was there, and she said he looked like a very cool fellow, and Yogi said, "You don't look so hot yourself."

Nixon's first love, after politics, was football. His fondness for the players and the sport was a mixture of genuine interest and practical politics. Accepting an award from the National Football Foundation, Nixon paraphrased the message of the first man on the moon, declaring:

I can only say that as far as this award is concerned, that it is a small step for football, but it is a giant leap for a man who never even made the team at Whittier.

160

Nixon liked to use sports phrases and metaphors to describe his political actions more colorfully, as when he referred to his Watergate battles as "playing hard-ball." At a testimonial dinner for pro quarterback Bart Starr of the Green Bay Packers, Nixon said:

> In my profession of politics, I got into the Super Bowl twice and only broke even. . . . I found that Bart Starr and I have something in common. I spent a lot of time on the bench and so did he. . . . A word about your Secretary of Defense [Melvin Laird]. I think it's only proper to speak of him in this room where all of us who follow football know that the defense is essential if you're going to be able to win the game.

Nixon thought he possessed gifts of prophecy in football and never tired of picking the winner of the upcoming season. Addressing a student-faculty convocation at the University of Nebraska, Nixon said:

> I want you to know that I have gotten into a little trouble over the past couple of years in picking number one teams. You will remember that before the bowl games I said that Texas was number one, and since then I have never been able to go to Pennsylvania without a passport.
>
> I was in Omaha in the last weeks of October. At that time Nebraska was number three in the Associated Press poll. And I had already been to Columbus, Ohio, where everybody said Ohio State was number one. I was in Indiana where everybody told me that Notre Dame was number one. I was in Texas where everybody told me that Texas was number one, and I was going to be in California. Of course, all Californians thought that Stanford was number one. And in Arizona, Barry Goldwater said Arizona State was number one.
>
> So I said to [Senator] Carl Curtis, "What should I do?"
>
> He thought a bit and said, "You know, Mr. President, I would wait until after the bowl games."

When Nixon accepted a plaque in his honor that would be mounted at the University of Nebraska, he said, "I shall now read the plaque which I understand will be put in one of the lockers."

Nixon was not America's happiest president and so there was often an undercurrent of bitterness in his humor, even on the most festive occasions, as when he said to the Football Hall of Fame banquet:

> This is a very special occasion for me because football is perhaps my second vocation. It is true that I have said I would like to have the Commissioner's job. . . . Would he like to have mine?

Chapter 21

Nixon Versus the Press

"I have said that if I had my life to live over again, I would like to be a sports writer. The trouble is, I could never make the deadlines."
RICHARD M. NIXON

The above wish for the life of a newspaper reporter was one of Nixon's rare sympathetic references to the press. His attitude toward newsmen, and the quality of humor he directed toward them, was generally abrasive. Perhaps as long as the republic endures, presidents and press will hold adversarial positions and the former will mask their hostility toward the latter behind a curtain of wit.

When Nixon assumed the presidency his compulsive sense of order was outraged by the cramped facilities of the White House press room. Since he rarely used the White House swimming pool, he had it transformed into a new White House press room. Many of the reporters resented being deprived of their old quarters, much as one misses a pair of battered old slippers, but Nixon was determined to have a facility that would let journalists cover him efficiently and perhaps even favorably. When he addressed the press corps at the ribbon-cutting ceremonies for its new quarters, some of the hostility that Nixon felt toward the media was discernible in this exchange:

163

BARNETT HORNER [Washington Star]. Mr. President, I think we should thank you for your interest in seeing that we get these new press quarters.

THE PRESIDENT. You are in the deep end of the pool right now. . . . I want you to know that I conceived the idea much to the distress of Mr. Ehrlichman. He is the only swimmer on the White House staff, and he said he has gained ten pounds since we closed the pool. . . . Where you are now covers up the pool area, and beyond there were two massage rooms, and a women's dressing room and a men's dressing room. I don't know where the Associated Press is.

RONALD ZIEGLER. It is in the men's room.

Richard Nixon's long-standing image of himself was of a man of principle constantly attacked by a dissembling press. Remarks about the media's fidelity to fact infested his remarks on any given subject. In speaking to the White House Conference on the Future of the Industrial World, Nixon said, "As you probably have noted in the press—and this report in the press is accurate—"

Nixon's animus toward the press fed on the leaks that found their way into print. This obsession led to the formation of "the plumbers," which triggered Nixon's downfall and disgrace. His antipathy to leaks emerged in veiled sarcasm, as at a staff meeting in early 1971 when Nixon said:

What I present this year in the State of the Union address will be by far the most comprehensive, the most far-reaching, the most bold program in the domestic field ever presented to an American Congress. We began to pour the coal on six months ago after we met in San Clemente, and I made the basic decisions. As you know, they were made then. That was a pretty well-kept secret. I didn't read it until the afternoon papers.

Nixon's distaste for the press and his propensity for the scatological were both apparent in a remark he made when he was asked about the media's tendency to put the President "under a microscope." Replied Nixon, "I don't mind a microscope, but when they use a *proctoscope* ..."

Nixon's attitude toward the press was even more vitriolic than that of Lyndon Johnson. At a meeting with his newly appointed Cabinet, Nixon declared:

> Always remember, the men and women of the news media approach this as an adversary relationship. The time will come when they will run lies about you, when the columnists and editorial writers will make you seem to be scoundrels or fools or both, and the cartoonists will depict you as ogres. Now, don't let this get you down—don't let it defeat you. Treat the press as ladies and gentlemen.

Henry Kissinger has observed that even a paranoid has enemies, and there is little doubt that the press hostility that Nixon resented actually existed in many quarters. Evidence of this mutual antagonism could be found in an exchange between Nixon and Dan Rather, when he was the White House correspondent for CBS. Rather's distaste for the President was well known to the Washington press corps and so, when he was recognized by Nixon at a press conference, and the reporter said, "Mr. President, Dan Rather of CBS News," a rumbling noise filled the room. There was some applause and some boos.

Said Nixon, "Are you running for something?"

Said Rather, "No, sir ... are you?"

On another occasion, Rather began his question by saying, "Mr. President, I want to state this question with due respect to your office—"

"That would be unusual," said Nixon.

In the midst of the Watergate melee, Rather asked the following explosive question: "Mr. President, I wonder if you could share with us your thoughts when you hear people who believe in you say, reluctantly, that perhaps you should resign or be impeached."

165

Replied Nixon dryly, "Well, I'm glad we don't take the vote in this room. . . ."

Though Richard Nixon directed a biting humor at members of the press, on at least one occasion he let down his hair before them in a display of antic humor that was almost vaudevillian.

President Nixon and Vice-President Spiro Agnew participated in a musical-comedy routine at the press's annual Gridiron Dinner. The event was described in all its surrealist splendor by Harold Brayman in his joyous review of evenings at the Gridiron, *The President Speaks Off the Record.*

Nixon appeared on the stage and took note of the journalists' songs and sketches that had satirized his disagreements with his vice-president. Nixon scowled in mock irritation and summoned Agnew to the stage.

"They seem to imply," frowned Nixon, "that you don't go along with me on all phases of government policy. . . . What about the 'southern strategy'?" Nixon referred to a political gambit intended to win southern support to the GOP.

"Mistuh President," drawled Agnew, "ah agrees with you completely!"

Whereupon a pair of pianos appeared.

"Tonight," said Nixon, "I will play the songs that were the favorites of some of our former presidents." He began with FDR's trademark song, "Home on the Range." But a moment later Agnew drowned him out with "Dixie."

Next Nixon fingered the melody of Truman's "Missouri Waltz," only to have it buried once again in the strains of "Dixie." By now the audience of journalists was in an uproar. Forgotten for the moment were Agnew's frequent and ferocious attacks on the media.

Once more Nixon went to the well, this time with LBJ's "The Eyes of Texas Are Upon You." And once again Agnew drowned it with "Dixie."

Nixon rose with dignity, took a Jack Benny pause, and said

to his rebellious Veep: "This is your last chance! This happens to be *my* favorite song. . . ." Nixon proceeded to play "God Bless America," and this time Agnew joined him in four-handed unison, with the entire audience rising to join the leaders in song.

And thus ended the Gridiron Dinner of March 1970, with a warm spirit of fellowship suffusing the air and linking press and president.

Certainly no one in the room could have foreseen that within three years both of the entertainers would have been forced out of office by the exertions of the audience.

Part Five
LYNDON B. JOHNSON

"Give me some jokes for my statement on behalf
of retarded children."
LYNDON B. JOHNSON

Chapter 22
Earthy Humor

"One story he wanted to use in a speech was about a bathroom that was being painted, and the lady of the house called downstairs, 'Yoo-hoo, Mr. Painter, come up and see where my husband put his hand this morning.' And the painter said, 'No thanks, I'm kind of tired, but I'll split a beer with you.'"

GEORGE REEDY

Lyndon B. Johnson's sense of humor can be assessed by a story that he never tired of telling with cruel relish. It did not always entertain his audience but it said much about what he thought was funny. He would recall a dinner for party leaders where he had been seated on the dais, Harry Truman to his right, Adlai Stevenson to his left. "In the course of the speech," said LBJ, "I made a low bow to Truman, and in the same motion I managed to push my ass within an inch of Adlai's face!" The anecdote and the act were emblematic of the Johnson humor—crude, cruel, physical, gratuitous.

"What humor he had was crude and coarse," reflected George Reedy, his former press secretary. "He could create witty turns of phrase, but most could not be repeated in polite company. Like his famous line about J. Edgar Hoover—'I'd rather have him inside the tent pissing out than outside the tent pissing in.'"

Ted Sorensen told me a Johnson crack that was typical of his marriage of wit and crudity.

171

"When he became vice-president," said Sorensen, "Johnson thought he would continue to be a power on Capitol Hill. Then he attended a caucus and was practically ignored. As he stormed out he said to an aide, 'Now I know the difference between a caucus and a cactus. With a cactus the pricks are on the *outside*.' "

"He had an excellent sense of mimicry," recalled George Reedy, "but it was basically cruel. He would do an impression of anyone he didn't like—Adlai Stevenson, Bobby Kennedy, some senator who was giving him trouble. He had a talent for mimicry which was quite distinctive—you'd swear they were right there. But most of his humor was crude."

Johnson was not the well of rustic humor that his biographers would suggest. "Most of the time you had to beat jokes out of him," said Reedy. "To me a sense of humor is a sense of proportion and *that* he didn't have. Not in the sense that Stevenson and Kennedy had a sense of humor. If you examined the humor in his speeches you'd see they had one of two objectives—either to put a point across or as an expression of hate."

The custodians of the Johnson Museum in Austin, Texas, have struggled to humanize and civilize Lyndon Johnson in the eyes of scholars and historians. The effort is ultimately futile. LBJ was too raw and his humor too bawdy to permit a portrait of the polite populist to emerge. Johnson was powerful, manipulative, and even magnificent, but he was mean and petulant as well, and these qualities are more evident than magnanimity in his humor.

There were other examples of the Johnson boorishness that George Reedy recalled in his evocative book *Lyndon B. Johnson: A Memoir*. There was the occasion when Johnson hoisted the tail of his shirt to reveal a long, searing scar on his belly to White House cameras. There was the state luncheon when Johnson seized some food off the plate of a diplomat's startled wife. There was the occasion when he told his assembled staff the kind of fidelity he expected from them. "I expect," said the President, "a kiss-my-ass-at-high-noon-in-Macy's-window loyalty." Whether any of his counselors were ever put to this ultimate test has gone unreported.

Mark Antony to the contrary, the evil that men do does *not* always live after them, and it has become traditional to shrug off Johnson's barnyard jokes and loutish manners with the observation that he was, after all, a simple man who lived close to the soil. It should be noted that there is little soil in Washington and that is where Johnson spent his adult life.

It is a more credible theory that LBJ's crudities flowed not from his humble birth but from a calculated desire to shock and subdue. There is a tyrannical mischief to a man who behaves loutishly for the pleasure of watching fastidious people pretend not to mind.

One of the fastidious folk who had to pretend they weren't offended by Johnson's uncivilized manners was John Kenneth Galbraith, a product of Harvard and establishment breeding. Galbraith later recalled Jack Kennedy's reaction to Johnson's profanities. Kennedy was no Puritan where humor was concerned and would exchange ribald stories with his intimates, but Johnson was a bit much for Kennedy's taste. Said Galbraith of the Johnson humor: "Kennedy was revolted by it. He was not amused by vulgar language. . . ."

Few of Johnson's aides had the temerity to try to censor the presidential humor, though many were tempted to do what George Reedy did on an occasion when Johnson started to tell a particularly tasteless joke. Said Reedy, "I had to put my hand over his mouth to keep him from telling it."

One of Johnson's oldest friends and staunchest advocates insists that he was not a crude man. "He was not vulgar. A product of the barnyard, yes, but not vulgar." This is a distinction that leaves one glassy-eyed. It is acknowledged by those closest to him that Johnson could be a mite indelicate, as when he paused to scratch his behind in public, or clawed at an obstruction in his nose, or carried on a nonstop conversation while urinating in the Oval Office bathroom. Jack

Valenti, Johnson's senior aide and presently guardian of moviemakers' morals as ruler of the motion picture rating code, insists that Johnson was not "coarse," he was "earthy." Valenti came to Johnson's service from the field of advertising so he is accustomed to presenting the product in the most appealing light.

There was often a sexual undertone to the Johnson humor. Referring to Nixon's economic policies, Johnson snapped, "They're the worst thing that's happened to this country since pantyhose ruined finger-fucking."

But LBJ exercised a double standard in his humor—he was careful to sanitize his speech in the company of women. In the presence of his wife he was positively puritanical. There were notable exceptions to this rule of respect for the fair sex, as when he lowered his trousers to show some startled White House secretaries the site of a hernia injury.

Johnson's speech was ripe with sex and scatology. A colorful colloquialism for coercion was "I've got his pecker in my pocket." His similes would never make the Picturesque Speech pages of the *Reader's Digest*. A sample from the Johnson repertoire: "It was raining as hard as a cat pissing on a flat rock." Johnson also had a gift for metaphor: "I may not know much, but I do know the difference between chicken shit and chicken salad."

In Johnson's defense it must be said that he was a masculine man in a society that was growing less masculine, in a city where macho traits were rare and sensitivity was highly prized. In the evenhanded appraisal of one journalist, "He was a very big man—with equivalent faults."

Frank Cormier, the highly respected White House correspondent for the Associated Press, recalled some of Johnson's earthy quips in his engaging book *LBJ—The Way He Was*.

"You fellows know what a steer is," Johnson told a group at his ranch. "That's a bull who's lost his social standing."

Lyndon once declared, "What we have to do is take the bull by the tail and look the situation in the face."

Addressing a session of Congress that had acted on most of the legislation he had sent them, he said, "I am reminded of that old song we used to sing in the hills of Texas, 'Keep on doin' what you're doin' to me, because I like what you're doin' to me.' "

Johnson's risqué humor was often immensely appealing and terribly funny. On the campaign trail in 1964, Johnson told this story to a women's group:

> Someone brought a big black bulldog into a neighborhood and pretty soon the whole neighborhood was flourishing with little black dogs, very much to the distress of the ladies of the neighborhood. They decided to do something about it and they consulted a veterinarian. And they took the dog in and had him operated on. Well, there was relative calm in the community for a period of two or three years. And pretty soon the dogs started flowering again, puppies were waddling down all the sidewalks. And the Ladies Aid Society met and were discussing it, and one old lady said, "I'll tell you what's happened! It's that damned black bulldog. That's what's causing it all." And the other lady observed, "Well, I thought we had him operated on." And the first lady said, "I know, but he's acting as a consultant."

But Johnson's public humor could not hold a candle to his private obscenities. Frank Cormier recalled some of them with relish.

When opposition to the Vietnam War grew in scope and volume, Johnson said he felt like a mongrel bitch assaulted by a pack of males: "If I run, they chew my tail off. If I hunker down, they fuck me to death."

When Sargent Shriver was proposed as a possible running mate, Johnson hunched forward, reached back between his legs, grabbed his buttocks, and said, "Sarge Shriver couldn't find his ass with both hands!"

When Lyndon Johnson visited a pocket of poverty in the Kentucky hills and encountered a poor soul paralyzed below the waist, the President was delighted at the man's radiant response. "Did you see that little ol' boy when he looked up and saw his President? There was a satisfied man. It reminded me of my old daddy's definition of the satisfied man. He's the fellow that takes a good healthy shit every mornin'—and gets his newspaper on time."

If that colorful aphorism has a familiar ring it is because eleven years later a racist version of that remark by Secretary of Agriculture Earl Butz led to his resignation and disgrace.

Much of Johnson's humor revolved around the genitourinary tract. After LBJ had demolished Barry Goldwater at the polls, he herded a group of newsmen around his ranch and showed them the spot where his bones would some day rest. "If Goldwater had won, there's where I'd be right now," he exclaimed. Then he unzipped his fly and urinated on the gravesite.

When *Life* estimated Johnson's wealth at fourteen million dollars, the President seethed. "I was swimmin' in the White House pool with those fellows from *Life* a few weeks ago and we weren't wearin' any suits," said Johnson. "But how in hell could they claim that my pecker is fourteen inches long if they didn't actually measure it!"

When José Mora, the secretary-general of the Organization of American States, extricated Johnson from a potential quagmire in Santo Domingo to which LBJ had dispatched U.S. troops, he was full of gratitude. Said Johnson, "That José Mora did such a wonderful job, he can have everything I've got! He can have my little daughter Luci. Why, I'd even tongue him myself!"

Chapter 23
The Humor Group

"The best humor is when it comes out of the
earth that shapes you."
—LIZ CARPENTER

"Tell Liz to keep sending me jokes!" commanded Lyndon
Johnson.

Liz Carpenter was LBJ's chief comedy writer in the White
House, and she assembled a group of after-hours wits from the
Johnson speechwriting staff to add humor to his pronounce-
ments.

Liz had grown up in Texas, come to Washington in 1942,
and promptly called on her congressman—who happened to
be Lyndon Johnson.

A reporter by trade, she worked for the leading paper in the
district Johnson represented. When she married an Austin
boy, the Johnsons came to the wedding.

"You know Texans are very clannish," laughed Liz.

She covered LBJ as his political star continued to rise—
from congressman to senator to the Senate majority leadership.

When Jack Kennedy shocked his disciples by choosing
Johnson as his vice-presidential running mate, LBJ asked Liz
to take some time off from her reporting to travel with Lady
Bird and assorted Kennedy women on the campaign trail.

"We were in Texas," said Liz, "proving to them that
Roman Catholics don't have horns."

177

After the victorious campaign, she went to work for LBJ.

"Because I had a gift for humor, he would hand me a speech and say, 'Sex it up,' by which he meant put some jokes at the beginning. Humor always improved him, because if you get some feedback from the crowd, you become a ham."

When Johnson assumed the presidency after the assassination of John Kennedy, his demands for humor escalated along with the frequency of his speeches.

"The Humor Group was my idea," said Liz, "because I think humor is contagious and a group is the best way to write humor—particularly in Washington, where humor is topical and we all could sit down, look at the headlines, and say, 'What are the key things that would lend themselves to humor this week?' "

The Humor Group would meet in Liz's East Wing office every Monday at five, and she enjoyed herself immensely.

"The meetings were marvelous—it was the best day of the week," she recalled.

"President Johnson had a whole stable of writers in the West Wing of the White House. There were scores of speeches and messages to be produced every week. You had everything from major addresses to what they indelicately called Rose Garden garbage. Johnson would have maybe twelve or fifteen remarks [short speeches] a day to groups that came through, from Red Cross workers to ministers. So they were pouring that stuff out. . . .

"So they would send a list of the speeches that he was going to deliver for the next week, and sometimes early drafts. And the list of where they would be. And we would meet and come up with introductions—humorous ways to get into the speech."

There were frustrations along with the fun. Liz Carpenter's comics would provide LBJ with a selection of jokes from which to choose.

"Sometimes he surprised us with his choices," recalled Liz. "Sometimes he really disappointed us. Some joke that we thought was a marvelous gag, he wouldn't use. It was too close to the skin."

Sometimes Liz was dismayed to learn that others were working on jokes for the same speech. "LBJ was a great one for giving ten assignments around the White House so that somebody would get it done. This was a frustrating thing because you'd like to think you were the only one."

There were others in the White House who were writing humor but Liz's was the key comedy group. "And he knew it," snapped Liz proudly.

Liz Carpenter was no respecter of organizational charts where her humor was concerned. "I am not a channel person," she told me. "It drives people crazy, but I am not. I didn't go to anybody. I had access to the second floor. I had been an old family friend. I could just go up and leave it on his bedside."

Any speechwriter with a penchant for fun joined the Humor Group. The volunteers numbered five or six, and the meetings were faithfully attended.

"Perhaps it was because Ernie Cuneo would always bring a bottle of Chivas Regal," laughed Liz.

As hostess of these assemblies, Liz moved a small cabinet into her office and stocked it with liquor and assorted mixers. In addition to bringing the Chivas Regal, Ernie Cuneo also brought a memory stocked with vintage stories he had written for Franklin Roosevelt.

At the appointed hour on Monday, Liz's office resembled a writers' conference at *Saturday Night Live*, though a similar irreverence was not encouraged.

Liz recalled the meetings in her lively memoir *Ruffles and Flourishes*. She would sit huddled over her manual typewriter, which rested on a coffee table in the center of the room. The gaggle of gagwriters would mix their drinks and position themselves about the room in attitudes conducive to humor and thought.

There was the bespectacled Peter Benchley, who had not yet discovered the financial potential of sharks. His family boasted a distinguished tradition in humor in the short essays of his grandfather Robert Benchley.

"Peter always suggested the wrong kind of humor for Johnson," recalled Liz. "It was more suited to Martha's Vineyard. The best humor is when it comes out of the earth that shapes you."

(It was Peter Benchley who refused to leave a dinner party when summoned to work on a Johnson speech, prompting the President to say, "Fire him!" Joe Califano came to Benchley and said, "The President wants you fired," and Benchley replied, "Well, if the President wants me fired, the President will have to fire me." Califano returned to the President and said, "Mr. President, he won't leave." LBJ felt it was beneath his dignity to fire a mere speechwriter, so Benchley remained till the end of Johnson's term.)

Another valuable member of the Humor Group was Ben Wattenberg, who was to write a major portion of Johnson's famous Gridiron speech at Williamsburg, Virginia.

Ervin Duggan was "boyish as a choirboy," recalled Liz. He perched on the edge of a chair, ready to explode in comedic inspiration.

Then there was Joe Laitin, chain-smoking and grinning mischievously. Laitin once received a phone call from the President announcing that he was going to address a group of retarded children in the Rose Garden and needed some humor. Dismayed, Laitin told George Reedy his assignment. "What can I do?" asked Laitin. Said Reedy, "Tell him to say, 'I love retarded children. I used to be one myself.'"

The air was filled with smoke and one-liners struggling to be born. Occasionally a secretary would be dispatched for more ice. The orders were "No calls except the President."

By seven P.M. a draft of the best jokes would be messengered to a Johnson aide who would rush them to the President, who in turn would approve those he liked and deep-six those he didn't.

The temptation to rewrite comedy is irresistible, as any Hollywood writer knows to his grief, and the Humor Group's intermediary sometimes took to "improving" the jokes that passed through his hands. Miss Carpenter bridled. Henceforth she ignored channels and handed the fruits of her wit to Johnson's valet to give the President before he retired. Johnson never lacked for light bedtime reading, at least on Monday evenings.

After the first few weeks, the demands on the Humor Group members increased. It was their task to fulfill the ever-growing needs of their presidential patron. He had heard the laughter and found it good. Soon the group was meeting not once but twice a week to meet the expanding Johnson demands for humor.

Soon the corridors of power were ringing with encomiums to the comedy claque. Vice-President Hubert Humphrey, a man with a robust taste for comedy, called on the East Wing wags for material. Several Cabinet members put in requests for lampoonery relevant to their own departments. Betty Furness, who had just been named Johnson's adviser for consumer affairs, turned to the group for jokes, perhaps missing the comforting prop of a refrigerator. Lest it be thought that the whole ballooning operation was taking on the aspect of a Marx Brothers comedy, it must be recalled that the Carpenter group was creating comedy in the national interest.

The jokes that were rejected by the President as undeserving of his august office were passed on to Vice-President Humphrey, whose position did not permit such discrimination.

This led to an exquisite terror for Liz Carpenter. She recalled, "I lived in constant fear that some night on the same platform, Johnson and Humphrey would end up with the same lines."

The Humor Group reached its zenith when it provided Lyndon Johnson with a complete speech of one-liners for delivery at the Gridiron Club. According to speechwriter Horace Busby, Johnson resisted attending the Gridiron affairs. "He felt it was inappropriate for a President to be making funny speeches. That wasn't good form." Busby reflected a moment and added derisively, "Of course Reagan does it. Hell, Reagan has been the President at a thousand roasts!"

Johnson was invited to address the Gridiron Club when the annual dinner was in historic Williamsburg. This time he accepted, and his Humor Group leaped into action. Given Johnson's incapacity for self-deprecation, his antagonism toward the press, and his distaste for sullying the presidential purple with jokes, it was a daunting assignment. On top of these problems was the fact that the Johnson stock was falling fast with the public and press. American campuses were exploding in antiwar sentiment, casualty figures were mounting, and Johnson was pouring more troops into an increasingly dubious war. Could humor retrieve such a calamitous state of affairs?

In addition, Johnson was uncomfortable in the knowledge that he would be judged against the high standards established by John F. Kennedy, who had dazzled the journalists with his coruscating wit. Johnson was coruscating on thin ice.

At the Gridiron Dinner, Johnson squirmed through a series of skits and songs in which newsmen mocked his warts and weaknesses. Johnson had little tolerance for criticism, sardonic or otherwise, but he laughed the hollow laugh of the condemned. The show ended with the customary toast to the President.

Johnson's first line was: "I enjoyed the skits—I think."

LBJ was looking ahead to the 1968 elections with increasing trepidation. He had not as yet declared that he would not seek reelection, and a covey of Republicans were potential opponents. He set his sights on one of these, auto magnate George Romney:

> I've been out with the troops the last two days [he said] and I
> didn't know until I got in tonight that as a result of the new

automobile safety regulations, the Rambler had already called in George Romney.

The laughter was encouraging and Johnson expanded his target to include Richard Nixon, who was another highly visible opponent in the forthcoming campaign:

Ever since I ran off to California when I was a boy and I washed cars out there for a living—that was before I ever met Nixon or Romney—it seems like I've always been having lots of trouble with these used car fellows.

Then, reminding the reporters of Nixon's bitter declaration to the press that this was his last press conference and that they would not have Nixon to kick around anymore, Johnson smiled:

I said to Lady Bird the other night, "Tell me, won't Nixon have a credibility problem if he should be President, not ever being able to hold another press conference?"

The joke also referred to Johnson's own credibility problem, which he had created by dissembling about the extent of U.S. involvement in Vietnam and the prospects of victory. Johnson then referred to the historic site of their dinner:

Political tradition began in this city. It was here in Williamsburg that George Washington, our first President, constantly reminded about his credibility, made the first news leak in American history. It was a story about a boy and a cherry tree and it ended with a line no White House reporter would ever buy today. He said, "I cannot tell a lie."

The public was turning against Johnson, and his decline would soon climax when he nearly lost the New Hampshire primary to Senator Gene McCarthy and decided not to run for reelection. But at this point the proud Johnson was still contemptuous of polls. He concluded:

The statesmen of Williamsburg were some of our first political animals, and it was here that a special courier first delivered the advance release which referred to Patrick Henry's private poll from his home district: "46 percent for liberty, 39 percent for death, 15 percent undecided."

There is an inevitable analogy to be drawn between the Johnson Humor Group and the system of committee writing that has evolved in the creation of Hollywood comedy.

Beginning with Norman Lear and *All in the Family*, most sitcoms have become the product of a group of writers rather than merely one.

It was discovered by Lear and his disciples that when you bring a number of witty sensibilities to bear on the same script, the comedy that issues forth is more abundant. Any loss in the unity of style is compensated for in the wealth of comedy you produce. The star can impose a unity in the performance.

In the same way, Lyndon Johnson preferred his humor, like almost everything else, in wholesale lots. He would unify it with the force of his personality.

The similarities between television comedy and Johnsonian humor suggested a growing kinship between the products of Hollywood and Washington, one that would reach its zenith fifteen years later in the election of our first actor-president.

Chapter 24
The Folksy President

"Lyndon Johnson was one of the best storytell-
ers I ever met and his fund of tales was rich."
FRANK CORMIER,
LBJ—The Way He Was

To the public, Lyndon Johnson was a genial, beaming, patri-
archal president.

He tried to present himself to the electorate as a benign,
folksy product of the Texas hill country, a man of simple
tastes and Lincolnesque wisdom.

He was a splendid storyteller and had a sizable reservoir of
stories, many of them centering on the Pedernales River and
the Texas hills where he had grown to manhood.

He knew how to weave his stories into his speeches in an
adroit fashion that should have endeared him to the public
and won its allegiance, trust, and affection.

Why didn't the Johnson humor work?

Unfortunately for LBJ, a man of Bunyanesque appetites
and parliamentarian brilliance, he came to the presidency in
the beginning of the Age of Television and he was a man who
grew tense under the unrelenting glare of the camera's eye.
Thus the public—the vast millions who saw him only on the
black-and-white TV tube—was never entirely beguiled by his
bucolic charm.

185

Lyndon Johnson had been raised in the rural tradition of long-winded speeches. The South has produced many great orators who have thrilled our forebears on countless Fourth of July celebrations and Johnson spoke in that tradition. In the hill country of Texas, oratory offered an excellent chance for entertainment and education.

But television had trained us to expect our entertainment in fast gulps. America's most popular comedy show would soon be *Laugh-In*, with its rapid pace and frenetic cutting. John Kennedy's humor was generally quick and crisp, as would be the humor of Ronald Reagan, twenty years later.

The stories Lyndon Baines Johnson spun out on the stump would not go over well on the television medium, which has to be a second home to the chief executive. On TV, humor and news come in quick bites.

But those who saw LBJ in person and listened to his folksy stories were warmed by the man. He told one audience that we Americans like our democracy so much, we want everyone to have a taste of it—and of course there was a story to make the point:

> It's like the fellow [he said] who had a few too many drinks. He came home and he got to sleep and woke up in the middle of the night. His mouth was burning and he said to his wife, "Get me some ice water." And she got the pitcher of ice water and brought it to him and he took a drink. Then he said, "Honey, this is so good, go wake up the kids and give them some of it."

Johnson once began a speech in a manner that was certain to captivate with its homespun humor and humility. Upon receiving a lavish introduction from the governor of Michigan, LBJ said:

> I wish my mother and father might have been here to hear that introduction. My father would have enjoyed it, and my mother would have believed it.

Much of the public perceived Johnson as a calculating, backwoods politician, bent on seducing them with his bogus charm. To them his vast store of preacher stories did not so much reflect the God-fearing environment in which he was raised as a calculated attempt to manipulate them with his transparent pieties. But those who heard these stories in person, rather than on the cold television tube, liked the man immensely.

One of Johnson's favorite preacher jokes concerned a clergyman who dropped his sermon notes while heading for church and couldn't lay hands on them before his hound dog chewed them to pieces.

> When the preacher went into the pulpit [said LBJ] he apologized to his congregation and said, "I am very sorry, today I have no sermon. I will just have to speak as the Lord directs. But I will try to do better next Sunday."

Another preacher story that was extremely effective before a live audience but that would seem rambling on television was related to the Friendly Sons of St. Patrick in New York City. Johnson said:

> It always makes me a bit wary to be the last speaker on any program. . . . I remember one time in my home country a preacher was vexed because one of his congregation always went to sleep in the midst of the sermon. One Sunday while he was giving the devil fits, sure enough his sleeping worshiper was snoring gently in the front row.
>
> The preacher determined he would fix this character and fix him once and for all. So in a whisper he asked the congregation, "All who want to go to heaven, please rise." As one man, they all got to their feet except the front-row dozer. He kept snoring on. Then the preacher shouted at the top of his voice, "All those who want to be with the devil, please rise!" The sleepyhead came awake with a start. He jumped to his feet. He saw the preacher standing tall and angry in the pulpit, and he

said, "Well, preacher, I don't know what it is we are voting on, but it looks like you and me are the only ones for it."

Many citizens perceived Johnson as a man from whose simple country wisdom they could learn and the nation could profit. He was, after all, driving through Congress all the social legislation that his charismatic predecessor had merely talked about. Yet much to Johnson's vexation, he could never acquire the public adoration that belonged irretrievably to John F. Kennedy.

Lynda Bird Johnson used to say that had her father not gone into politics, he would have made a great raconteur. He could have made a nice living, she said, traveling about telling tales of the Texas hill country.

Harry Middleton, his onetime speech and humor writer and presently the director of the LBJ Museum in Austin, observed that Johnson used his stories to make a point because he was at heart a teacher.

Indeed, examples of these Johnsonian anecdotes fill an audiocassette that is a hot seller at the Johnson Museum. In these stories spun out in the rolling style of Lyndon Johnson, he is once more on the stump, hypnotizing the crowds:

During the early days of the Depression, a poor schoolteacher in search of a job applied to a school board. The board was rather impressed by his presentation. He was eloquent, he was factual, he was impressive. So the members of the board said to him, "Well, we think we would like to have you teach and we would like to retain your services. But tell us this: There is some difference of opinion in our community about geography, and we want to know which side you're one. Do you teach that the world is round or do you teach that the world is flat?" The applicant responded immediately, "I can teach it either way."

President Johnson told a group of business leaders an anecdote to explain why large funds were necessary for the missile race with the Russians:

In 1861, a Texan left to join the rebels. He told his neighbors he'd return soon, that the fight would be easy "because we can lick those damyankees with broomsticks." He returned two years later, minus a leg. His neighbors asked the tragic, bedraggled, wounded man what happened: "You said it'd be so easy, that you could lick the damyankees with broomsticks." "We could," replied the rebel, "but the trouble was the damyankees wouldn't fight with broomsticks."

When American troops were bogged down in a stalemated war in Vietnam, Johnson used this story to demonstrate the virtues of the situation:

It seems that Mark Twain was walking down a country road seeking the home of a friend. He stopped and asked a farmer how far it was and was told it was a mile and a half. Twain walked a little further, asked the same question and was told it was a mile and a half. This happened three more times. Finally Twain said, "Well thank God, I'm holding my own."

At a White House dinner, Johnson urged a group of businessmen to keep profits down, and vowed to ask labor leaders to do the same with wages. Said LBJ:

I will lay the cards out just as straight for them as I do for you. That way everyone will know the score—like the conversation at the card game when one of the boys looked across the table and said, "Now Reuben, play the cards fair. I know what I dealt you."

When Johnson asked a close friend for a candid assessment of the image he projected on television he received the unsettling reply, "It's a cross between Machiavelli and a riverboat gambler."

In formal surroundings—at a state dinner, before a joint session of Congress, under the eye of a TV camera—he was undone. But on the stump—with his colorful stories sliding off his tongue—the air of contrivance vanished. Johnson talked

189

the language of the people and became one of them. In those surroundings, LBJ was speaking to "the folks."

One of Johnson's most instructive and amusing stories was intended to tell his audience how great were his goals for America:

> I feel very much like Winston Churchill felt [he would say] when the ladies of the Temperance Union called upon him in the dark days just before the end of World War Two. And this disapproving lady said, "Mr. Prime Minister, we have it on reliable authority that if all the alcohol and all the brandy you have drunk during this war could be emptied into this room it would come up to about here." And it was a big room and she held her hand up above her head—it was more than half of the room filled with brandy and alcohol.
>
> And Churchill looked at the floor and then he looked at the ceiling and then he kind of pondered, and he said, "My dear little lady, so little have we done . . ." And then he took her hand and looked at where it was measuring and saw how far it was to the ceiling and he said, "So much we have yet to do."

Johnson thought nothing of appropriating the anecdotes of other politicians. Horace Busby recalled the day LBJ had summoned his agency heads to the East Room of the White House to speak with them about the budget. "The budget director was presiding," said Busby, "and Johnson was sitting in the corner next to me. Suddenly he turned to me, realizing he would have to say a few words to get things started, and said, 'Quick, Buzz, I need a good story to start.' And I said, 'Train wreck.' And he said, 'Train wreck? What train wreck? Start it for me!' " Busby supplied Johnson with the beginning of a story that a congressman friend used to relate and the President quickly recalled it:

> There was the young Texas teenager [said Johnson] and they were building a railroad past his town, right past his front door, and he applied for a job with the crew. The foreman said

he'd have to pass an intelligence test. So he asked him a few questions and the boy answered them. Then the foreman said, "Here's the big one. You answer this and you've got a job. Suppose you're standing by the switch in front of your house and you look to the east and you see a locomotive huffing and puffing down the track at sixty miles an hour heading west. And you look west and you see another train coming at sixty miles an hour heading east down the same track. What would you do?"

And the boy said, "I'd go into the house and get my brother." And the foreman said, "Why on earth would you get your brother?" And the boy said, "Because he's never *seen* a train wreck."

Johnson's point was that if his agency heads couldn't bring him a budget under a hundred billion dollars, they were headed for one hell of a train wreck.

Johnson appropriated another story that was told him by speechwriter Bob Hardesty, and told it to raise derisive laughter about the Republican enemy. Said LBJ:

There was this old man who needed a heart transplant and there were three choices in hearts that were available. There was an eighteen-year-old athlete, a nineteen-year-old dancer, and a seventy-five-year-old banker. The patient asked the politics of the banker and was told he was a Republican. Learning this, he chose the banker's heart.

The transplant was successful, and people asked the man why he chose the seventy-five-year-old's heart in preference to those of the vigorous young men. And he said, "I wanted a heart that I knew had never been used."

During the years Lyndon Johnson was in the Oval Office, I was writing a TV program of political satire called *That Was the Week That Was*. Indeed, Johnson took office and the show took to the air almost simultaneously. Johnson was much on our minds and the focus of public attention.

The perception of LBJ by the writers on the show was critical and skeptical. We saw him as a sleight-of-hand artist whose rustic homilies were a sham.

Much of the electorate had similar doubts that could not be defused by the Johnson humor, as Kennedy had defused our doubts with wit. The public seemed to sense that the Kennedy humor was genuine, and suspected that Johnson's folksy humor was a smokescreen.

Looking back on Lyndon Johnson through the prism of twenty years of hindsight and history, we recall him as the man who drove us deep into the quicksand of Vietnam. He was also the man who achieved passage of Medicare and the Civil Rights law. But the war has soured our recollections.

When he appears in the film *The Right Stuff*, Johnson is painted as an overbearing, boorish politician of a most tasteless stripe.

Biographers have painted him as a man of ego and impatience who demanded loyalty and obedience of an extraordinary kind.

The public recalls him for his rustic humor and country ways, a man who might prefer to sleep under the stars. The coarseness is buried in the memories of White House insiders.

Chapter 25
A Sense of
Inadequacy

"As a human being, he was a miserable person—a bully, sadist, lout and egotist.... It may well be that this was a form of self-loathing...."

GEORGE REEDY

Lyndon Johnson had a propensity for practical jokes tainted with cruelty, and a favorite form of amusement was bringing some aristocratic Ivy Leaguer into his bathroom and conferring with him during evacuation.

For Johnson a feeling of inadequacy seemed to permeate his political career and produce this malicious streak in his humor. The sense of inadequacy became especially apparent when Johnson succeeded in the Oval Office a brilliant, buoyant young president who was surrounded by intellectuals, whose speeches were poetry in politics, and whose wit brought Wilde to Washington.

Johnson would have liked to inherit the love that many Americans felt for their fallen leader, John F. Kennedy. When he did not, it spawned a resentment that often took the form of hostile humor and that was thinly veiled by banter. Small wonder that LBJ used humor to wound, to mock, and to look down at those who were above him.

A philosopher said, "We are all in the gutter but some of us are looking at the stars." Lyndon Johnson's perspective was that of a boy born to poverty who was looking at the stars—waiting for his chance to repay them for their contempt. He was awed and intimidated by America's political blue bloods, but he did not genuflect to the Lodges and the Bundys. Rather he would strike out in mocking humor, whenever the opportunity allowed, at the products of the eastern establishment.

It is not surprising that Johnson's humor was so different from Kennedy's. The men were strikingly dissimilar. Ted Sorensen, the speechwriter who served both men, points out the differences in his book *The Kennedy Legacy*. Johnson was shrewd while Kennedy was open. Kennedy tried to persuade his adversaries; Johnson tried to punish them. Kennedy enjoyed laughing at his own flaws; Johnson found this impossible and any aide who attempted it would soon be gone.

Even Johnson's most loyal aide and advocate, Jack Valenti, acknowledged the distinction between the Johnson humor and the Kennedy wit in his splendid memoir on life with his volcanic boss, *A Very Human President*. Wrote Valenti:

> The chief executive who took John Kennedy's place in the White House had a tough act to follow when it came to grace and wit. . . . It would not be accurate to describe LBJ's stories as "wit" in the Kennedy sense. They were not.

Johnson would have liked to copy the effortless Kennedy wit but it was beyond him. So, unable to emulate those elegant grace notes, Johnson came to resent any signs of Ivy League polish. Johnson came to believe—perhaps with some justice—that no frontier Texan could be loved as Kennedy was, or capture the hearts of the establishment. These Ivy Leaguers despised him, or so he felt, for his speech, his clothes, his lack of suavity and breeding.

Some of Johnson's aides shared this Kennedy-envy, depreciating the soaring rhetoric and subtle humor. Said longtime

Johnson adviser Busby, "Ted Sorensen's device of writing poetic rhetoric—like 'Ask not what your country can do for you'—well, that just about made it. Maybe you could close a speech with that. But Kennedy's inaugural address was really too much!"

Johnson's insecurity was political as well as psychological. He had finally reached the pinnacle, after all those years of cunning on Capitol Hill, all the cloakroom machinations. And now, with the ultimate power in his hands, there was another Kennedy in the wings, and New Frontiersmen were whispering about a restoration with Bobby Kennedy.

During those years, Bobby would use antic wit to remind Johnson of his presence. In a memorable line written by his press aide Frank Mankiewicz, Bobby said: "I have no designs on the presidency, and neither does my wife, Ethel Bird."

President Johnson was not amused.

The jokes at Johnson's expense by Kennedy partisans were often wounding. Correspondent Merriman Smith reflected on the venom that flowed between the Johnson and Bobby Kennedy camps. Said Smith, "Bobby's friends have dinner at some Georgetown home and they're cracking jokes about Johnson and his country ways, and they don't realize that within hours every one of those jokes will be repeated to Johnson."

The anti-Johnson jokes followed a certain pattern, mixing arrogance and cruelty. They condemned Texans as a group. They mocked Johnson's taste; they ridiculed his barnyard humor, his accent, and his false geniality.

Bobby tried to draw some of the poison from the relationship with humor. Ted Sorensen recalled writing the following line for Bobby to deliver at the Gridiron Club:

All those stories [said Bobby] about President Johnson and me not getting along during my brother's years in the White House simply do not square with the facts. We started out during the Kennedy Administration on the best of terms—

friendly, close, cordial—but then, as we were leaving the Inaugural stands ...

The dark side of Johnson's humor was directed at the Beautiful People—the Georgetown elite that gave him no love and less support in his overpowering 1964 mandate.

"They won't accept me," Johnson would complain. "I guess I don't wear the right cologne."

Johnson liked to "put on" these Kennedy intellectuals, recalled Frank Cormier. He would purposely call canapés "ore-doves" and watch to see who would react with disdain. It was a way to separate friends from phonies. Johnson delighted in putting tight-lipped, buttoned-down intellectuals in embarrassing situations. He took them swimming naked in the White House pool and feasted on their discomfort. "I like to drop them on their aristocratic asses," said LBJ. "I got that great intellectual John Gardner in my pool swimming bare-assed naked!"

Johnson would mock his resident intellectual, Professor Eric Goldman. During his brief stay in the White House, Goldman was kept well away from the corridors of influence. Johnson would say sneeringly "That there is Lady Bird's intellectual. He is a real *in-tel-lec-shul*. And he belongs to Lady Bird."

When Lyndon Johnson was Jack Kennedy's vice-president, LBJ was constantly finding Bobby Kennedy's footprints on his ego. Bobby, thought LBJ, was scheming to make him appear absurd. Bobby might have said that nature had anticipated him.

Johnson feared that Bobby was trying to cut him from the ticket when Jack ran in 1964. Lyndon's fear trickled out in a line he spoke to a press dinner:

This is an old political town. The archeologists recently discovered an old plank here on which only two words were written: "Dump Jefferson."

President Kennedy was aware of his vice-president's anxiety and gloom. As Merriman Smith remarked, "Kennedy spends more time writing a birthday greeting to Lyndon than writing a State of the Union address."

One day early in his presidency, JFK brought his protocol chief into the Oval Office and said, "Listen—I want you to take care of the Vice-President. I want you to watch over him and see that he's not ignored. Because *I'm* going to forget. My *staff* is going to forget. We're *all* going to forget. And I want you to remember."

But during the Camelot years, Lyndon Johnson, who wished everyone to love him, squirmed under the negligence or contempt of all the President's men. The problem kept returning to the Oval Office where, as with more weighty matters, the buck stops. As Jack Kennedy remarked to Arthur Krock, "I don't know what to do with Lyndon. I've got to keep him happy somehow. My big job is to keep Lyndon happy."

Hugh Sidey summed up the Johnson humor of insecurity better than most when he told me:

Lyndon Johnson was so lacking in self-confidence that it was very difficult for him to chide himself. In those areas where he felt confident, legislation, the manipulation of people, he was a scream. But Lyndon Johnson never laughed at himself. You'd go in with him and your sides would ache for hours from his humor. But the fact is he didn't laugh at himself. He just couldn't kid himself.

Nor could he tolerate some third person making fun of his foibles. Pierre Salinger, the press secretary whom Johnson inherited from Jack Kennedy with the office, made the mistake of attributing to LBJ the same ability for self-amusement as his former boss, and suffered for it. During a visit to the Johnson Ranch, Salinger was amused by an Art Buchwald column that focused on Johnson's peccadilloes. In his innocence,

Salinger suggested that Johnson read it. At lunch, storm clouds drifted over the table where the President, Salinger, staff, and family sat.

"Somebody get me the *Herald Tribune*," commanded Johnson. "Pierre tells me that Art Buchwald has written a very funny column today."

The newspaper appeared and the President thrust it at Salinger.

"Read it aloud, Pierre, so we can all hear it," said Johnson.

The uncomfortable Salinger read the column aloud. It was greeted by stony silence.

When Salinger concluded, the President sent a chilly glance around the table.

"Anybody think that's funny?" he asked.

Johnson's insecurity fostered an ego that Sam Rayburn said was "double-dipped," as when LBJ returned to Air Force One after delivering the commencement address to the graduating class of the University of Michigan. He was aglow in the warm reception he had received. Frank Cormier recalled the exchange:

"Well, what did you think?" Johnson asked the reporters.

"You got a hell of a reception," said Cormier. "There were twenty-seven interruptions for applause."

"No, no," protested Johnson, "there were twenty-nine!"

Whereupon he called over Jack Valenti who, as instructed, had indicated each outburst of applause on his copy of the speech. There were indeed twenty-nine—but two of them had come after Johnson was introduced and when he finished speaking.

Johnson's speeches, like those of most presidents in the television age, were sprinkled with humor, but his vanity and insecurity did not permit him to acknowledge that all these comic gems did not spring from his own fertile wit.

Horace Busby wrote some of the best of the Johnson humor and later recalled an evening when he learned, to his horror, that his contributions to LBJ's "spontaneous humor" were being widely publicized. It was the night of the Johnson inaugural ball, and the TV cameras were broadcasting live from the Sheraton-Park Hotel. Said Busby:

> Johnson was due there. I arrived early. There was a stage and a mike and it was obvious to me that he would have to say something, some humorous remarks, and I knew nothing had been prepared for him. So I borrowed some hotel stationery, tore it into 4x6 sheets, went up on the podium to escape the throng, and started printing the things for him to say. I didn't realize that all the networks were zeroed in on me—with the zoom lenses right down on the paper I was printing on. Later when Johnson arrived I handed him the papers and said, "The first two pages are funny." He got up there and said his things— and the cameras again zoomed in on the papers to show it was what I had written for him to be spontaneously witty! Thank God he didn't see the shots of me earlier. He would have been furious!

Chapter 26
The Monarch
and the Press

"The God-damned press has lied about me
enough!"

LYNDON B. JOHNSON

Johnson did not especially understand the workings of the
press, as Kennedy had. He viewed them as an extension of his
official family, to be handled with a mix of bullying and manipulation, a cheerleading section to praise his accomplishments and be blind to his flaws.

Lyndon Johnson's hostility toward the press, born of his
sensitivity to their slightest reproach, manifested itself in a
hundred ways—but most often it was in humor.

Naturally enough, most Washington correspondents could
not supply Johnson's fragile ego with the constant obeisance it
required, and the result was a stream of thinly veiled hostility—venom disguised as wit—that flowed from the Texas
monarch to his journalistic Judases.

Addressing a group of historians, LBJ said:

I can assure you that at times, especially after I read the newspapers, I have strong urges to be a writer. In fact, I sometimes
think the press needs some new writers.

Johnson could be mean and petty in his needling of working newsmen. Late one afternoon, recalls Frank Cormier, LBJ was passing through the reception lobby in the White House West Wing—the spacious room where reporters relax between the crises of the press room. Seeing a reporter dozing on a sofa, Johnson jabbed him with a bony finger and sneered, "I'm mighty pleased to see that the Chicago Tribune is ever on the alert."

Entering the capital's National City Christian Church, where LBJ would pray when he was in Washington, Johnson pinned a reporter with his eyes and snapped, "Come on in. You need this more than I do."

When Ludwig Erhard, West Germany's chubby, cigar-smoking chancellor, paid a visit to the LBJ Ranch to enjoy some hunting and some Texas hospitality, Johnson introduced him to the press corps with these words:

Mr. Chancellor, in a few moments I am going to turn you over to the American press, and then I think you will know how the deer feel.

Outraged at a story in *The Wall Street Journal* that asserted the public was losing its fondness for Johnson, the President attacked both the problem and the reporter:

I wonder [he said] if any of you have been reading that piece on how the American people love me. I think everyone knows how the *Journal* reflects the views of the man on the street—Wall Street. Somebody told me that the writer of that article is free-lancing now for *True Romances*.

Johnson felt that reporters who printed stories reflecting opposition to his war policies were a pack of libelers. He resented the antipathy to the war of Senator J. William Fulbright and the eastern papers that closely followed Fulbright's committee hearings. Said Johnson bitterly:

201

> I wonder if you have seen the latest announcement from the
> Senate Foreign Relations Committee that it is going to hold
> hearings on the Viet Cong. I want to deny the rumor that they
> intend to start those hearings in the Editorial Room of the *New
> York Times*.

For a man who was so quick to mock his journalistic critics,
Lyndon Johnson had little tolerance for pain when the needle
was directed at him. During the thousand days when LBJ was
suffering the unaccustomed impotence of the vice-presidency,
his misery was acute. Some enjoyed his agonies and reporters
would ask derisively, "Lyndon who?" Johnson's sensitivity to
this form of sadistic humor can well be imagined.

> The first thing when a man is elected Vice-President [he said],
> you media fellas start talking about "Well, what happened to
> Lyndon? Where is Lyndon Johnson?" And the press plays it
> up, and it's cruel and inhuman. . . .

Johnson was quick to invoke the word "slander" on those
rare occasions when the Washington press corps departed
from its acquiescent and flattering treatment. He cried slander when a Washington columnist observed that Johnson
could not find anyone he could beat at golf. When aides gin-
gerly pointed out that this was true, Johnson growled, "It's
possible to slander a person and still tell the truth."

Johnson was capable of his own petty slanders, with his
comments about absent newsmen running the gamut from
churlish to vicious. Learning that a womanizing reporter from
a New York daily had arrived in Texas, Johnson sneered,
"The price of whores is going up in Austin." And when he was
told that a conservative columnist of whom he was not overly
fond had been seen in the vicinity, Johnson scowled, "See
him! I can *smell* him."

Johnson was admonished by his courageous press secretary,
George Reedy, that his treatment of the press was too abusive
and Johnson should try to retrieve their goodwill. So the Pres-

ident briefly replaced the stick with the carrot, inviting the reporters' wives and children to join them at a press conference
on the White House lawn. But in addressing the group, LBJ
could not resist inserting some darts in his opening comments:

> Friends and reporters—I hope you are the same—and children
> of reporters. I am so glad so many of you youngsters are here
> today. I want to prove to you that your fathers are really on the
> job—sometimes. I am glad your mothers came, too. I suspect
> they are very pleased to find your fathers working today.
>
> I thought you children deserved a press conference because I
> know that you have taken so many telephone calls for your fa-
> thers and mothers and located your wandering parents at so
> many receptions, that you have become good reporters too.
>
> When the press conference is over, I want to ask all the chil-
> dren to come up here and pose with me for a group picture.
> Let's don't have any mamas and papas. They are always
> crowding into pictures anyway.

Johnson's doctors had suggested daily exercise and so he
embarked on a regimen of six brisk daily laps around the pe-
riphery of the White House grounds. As the President walked,
his dogs would be yapping on a leash before him and a covey
of reporters would be scribbling in his wake. Johnson enjoyed
needling the correspondents about their inability to keep up.
At a ceremony in honor of physical-fitness award winners,
LBJ gestured to the nearby reporters and said sarcastically:

> You may not be able to tell it by just looking at them, but I
> want to give my personal testimony in behalf of the newspa-
> permen and newspaperwomen, that they are doing well in our
> own White House physical fitness training program on our
> daily walks. Of course, we have had a few casualties—we have
> lost one or two high heels, and had one or two dropouts. . . .

One story of the Johnson presidency rankled like no others.
It did not involve Vietnam, social progress, or human rights.
It dealt with Johnson's practice of hurtling through the hill

country at ninety miles an hour in his Lincoln Continental, with a can of beer cradled in his hand. When accounts of his recklessness hit the news wires, the President felt that the press had betrayed him.

The story, which first appeared in *Time*, described how he thundered across the Texas countryside, ogling the attractive newswoman beside him and ignoring the apprehensive newsmen behind him. LBJ was wounded by the story, which displayed several of his less laudable traits concurrently—his recklessness, his taste for spirits, and his eye for the ladies.

At first he tried to defuse the *Time* story with forced good humor, but the bitterness peeked through. Said Johnson:

> I wish to appoint a new commission to study what happened to the governor on my Lincoln Continental. It's supposed to keep me from going more than sixty-five miles an hour. The commission will be headed by Henry Luce.
>
> But until the report is in, there will be a new policy at the LBJ Ranch. Everybody walks—and drinks Pepsi-Cola.

Addressing the press at a Gridiron Dinner, Johnson's anger was more apparent. He was the offended party, he implied, since reporters who had been guests on his ranch had repaid his hospitality with betrayal. Said LBJ:

> After this evening—and some experiences of my own—I'm none too sure which is more hazardous: being a guest of the press or having the press as your guest.

Still chafing about the speed and alcohol story, Johnson struck a philosophic pose and said:

> Throughout my life I have determined that things usually happen for the best. For example, Lady Bird was flying to Cleveland the other day and her plane was struck by lightning. But even that had one salutary effect. Now she's willing to drive with me again.

A pattern emerged between the thin-skinned Johnson and the press. His behavior would produce a revealing story, Johnson would struggle to laugh it away with humor, he would fail, and then would turn bitter. This was the familiar course of events when the President raised a howl from animal lovers by lifting his pet beagles by their ears.

The cosmic event occurred in the Rose Garden when LBJ was playing with his daughter Luci's beagles, Him and Her. A group of financiers was present as the President hoisted the puppies by their ears. As the dogs yelped in pain, Johnson cracked, "You see what a dog will do when he gets in a crowd of bankers?"

When the Associated Press carried the story to hundreds of papers and produced a storm of criticism, Johnson protested that he had done the deed at the request of an AP cameraman—as though the President were so easily manipulatable.

The ear pulling was satirized by many. On *That Was the Week That Was*, we had Vice-President Humphrey saying, "I don't know what all the fuss is about. Lyndon lifts me that way all the time." But all the fuss continued to rankle Johnson throughout his days in office. He even found a way to lift the dogs by their ears without producing a yelp of pain, and demonstrated it to a group of reporters.

"See?" said Johnson. "He doesn't yelp unless an AP photographer gets too close."

LBJ never forgave the media for reporting the original story. Weeks later, he told some correspondents, "The day after I picked up that beagle by the ears, I picked him up again and I said to him, 'Son, don't you yelp or those reporter fellows will quote you.' "

Johnson could pay lip service to freedom of the press but it was usually conditional, recalling the bromides to the effect that one cannot be just a little pregnant and there is no such thing as a little garlic. Said Johnson on constraining the truth:

I don't expect to muzzle criticism. Every one of you say we invite free speech in our country and we want free speech and we
want criticism, don't we? Every one of you do. But there is a
limit to how much you want, and there is a ceiling on how
much is good for you.

Johnson's rage at the press reflected his extreme sensitivity,
even by presidential standards. It certainly did not reflect
journalistic abuse, since most Washington correspondents
outdid themselves in flattery and obeisance. One of the few
exceptions who were willing to regularly observe the Johnson
warts was James Reston, who wrote in his *New York Times* column, "Johnson is tyrannical with his personal staff, disorderly
about administration, apoplectic about characters who write
sentences like this ... more thin-skinned about criticism than
anybody since the last President Johnson. ... He has tended
to regard dissent as perversity, as if criticism were not a duty
in a free society but a crime."

Lyndon Johnson once described Washington as a city in
which the crucial question was: "Who is doing the fucking
and who is getting fucked."
    This crotch-level view of the Republic and its colorful artic-
ulation goes to the heart of the Johnson wit and philosophy.
    He was a combative man who viewed life as a battle to be
won, a woman as a citadel to be stormed, the press as an
enemy to be ruled with carrot or stick.
    Johnson's folksy humor was wrapped around the prickliest
ego in a city of massive egos. Anything short of subservience
was betrayal. Anything short of cheerleading was antagonism.
    Lyndon Johnson was an original. As one disgruntled hostess
remarked after he had dismayed her dinner guests with some
boorish behavior, "Before they made Lyndon Johnson they
broke the mold."

Part Six

JOHN F. KENNEDY

"Do we have any Republicans here today? . . . We
will have to be very careful what we say."
JOHN F. KENNEDY

Chapter 27
Defusing Issues

"I see nothing wrong with giving [Bobby] a little legal experience before he goes into private practice."

JOHN F. KENNEDY

When a lanky young senator from Massachusetts contrived to win the Democratic presidential nomination in the summer of 1960, he found himself burdened by some formidable problems:

1. He was unknown and facing a man who had debated Khrushchev, served Eisenhower, and sent Alger Hiss to prison.
2. His father was a financier whose wealth and power were resented by many.
3. He was a Roman Catholic whose religion raised fears that public policy might be dictated by the Vatican.
4. He was young, and surrounded by others who were even younger.
5. He was inexperienced in executive and legislative matters.

How on earth could such a young man capture the highest office in the land?

Most of these issues could not be faced directly with a battalion of facts. Youth, religion, wealth did not lend themselves to rational exposition. They were emotional matters where reason took a backseat to the viscera.

209

And so John F. Kennedy turned to humor.

It was a providential choice of weapons. Kennedy was, by temperament, armed with a wry, ironic wit. His chief speechwriter and most intimate aide, Ted Sorensen, along with an extraordinary gift for rhetoric, had a delicious sense of humor. Kennedy had the charisma, confidence, and timing to deliver comic lines.

Adlai Stevenson had made humor respectable in his losing campaigns of 1952 and 1956. As Sorensen observed, "Stevenson should get the credit for blazing the trail and making it easier for Kennedy's brand of humor to be accepted."

Of course, for Stevenson humor was freighted with risk. He was accused of dealing frivolously with weighty matters. Kennedy did not suffer this rebuff when he turned to wit. Said Hugh Sidey, "With Stevenson there was a whiff of arrogance." Said Sorensen, "The public liked and admired Kennedy more than they did Stevenson, and so what they regarded as trivialization coming from Stevenson, they regarded as sparkling personality coming from Kennedy."

Kennedy methodically used humor to laugh away each of the most troublesome issues he faced in the 1960 campaign.

His father's wealth enabled him to purchase a plane for campaigning and launch a well-financed campaign. But wealth is a double-edged sword. There was talk that Joe Kennedy was buying the election for his son. Kennedy proceeded to laugh the issue away with remarks like this:

I just received a telegram from my father. He says, "Don't buy one more vote than you need. I'll be damned if I'll pay for a landslide.

On another occasion Kennedy declared:

The Secretary of Commerce has announced a major new plan for restricting the outflow of gold to France—by keeping my father at home this year.

Kennedy's father could be a weighty cross to bear. He was known as a curt, ruthless, authoritarian businessman, and accounts of his harshness could hurt his candidate son. Unable to rebut the unflattering portrait, Kennedy chose to laugh at it. When one of the Kennedy sisters was married, a newspaper reported that one of Joseph Kennedy's executives had said with a smile that the wedding would cost in the hundreds of thousands. "Now I *know* that story is a phony," said Kennedy. "No one in my father's office smiles."

In defusing public animus toward his father's wealth, Kennedy would often add a needle to the wit, as when he was interrupted by a heckler who snarled, "I hear that your father has only offered two dollars a vote. With all your dough, can't you do better than that?" Kennedy snapped, "It's sad that the only thing you have to offer is your vote, and you're willing to sell that."

In a speech at Wittenberg College on ethics in government, Kennedy once again took antic aim at his father's bankbook. "Campaign contributions," he promised, "will not be regarded as a substitute for training and experience for diplomatic positions. . . . Ever since I made that statement, I have not received one single cent from my father."

Kennedy's religion was another formidable problem that could best be neutralized with humor. First Kennedy addressed the problem seriously in an eloquent speech to the Houston Ministerial Association. But a leavening of humor was needed to augment the oratory. And so Kennedy later said:

> I have asked Cardinal Spellman how to deal with the question of the Pope's infallibility. And Cardinal Spellman said, "I don't know what to tell you, Senator. All I can say is, he keeps calling me Spillman."

To make it clear to the electorate that he did not stand in awe of the Catholic Church and its distinguished leaders, he would sometimes laugh at their obesity and indulgences. At one dinner, standing beside an overweight churchman, he said:

> It is an inspiration to be here with one of those lean, ascetic clerics who show the effect of constant fast and prayer, and bring the message to us in the flesh.

Kennedy poked fun at his religion throughout the campaign. Former President Truman had resorted to some characteristic profanity in deriding the Republicans, and a sanctimonious Richard Nixon deplored the example that Truman was setting for the nation's youth. Said Kennedy:

> I would not want to give the impression that I am taking former President Truman's use of language lightly. I have sent him the following wire:

> Dear Mr. President: I have noted with interest your suggestion as to where those who vote for my opponent should go. While I understand and sympathize with your deep motivation, I think it is important that our side try to refrain from raising the religious issue.

By laughing at the religious question, Kennedy encouraged the irreverent press to join in the jollity. At one press conference a reporter asked, "Do you think a Protestant can be elected President in 1960?" Playing along, Kennedy replied:

> If he's prepared to answer how he stands on the issue of separation of church and state, I see no reason why we should discriminate against him.

Kennedy recalled another Catholic politician whose religion had denied him the White House, seeking to laugh the issue out of existence. Said Kennedy:

> Some circles invented the myth that after Al Smith's defeat in 1928 he sent a one-word telegram to the Pope: "Unpack."

After my press conference on the school bill [opposing aid to parochial schools] I received a wire from the Pope myself: "Start packing!"

Kennedy's youthful appearance was another problem that he chose to treat lightly. He used to tell audiences of the time when he was waiting in a Senate office building elevator, and "some people got in and asked me for the fourth floor."

The press speculated that the cortisone Kennedy took for an adrenal deficiency had the side effect of puffing out his face, perhaps the only time in American history when medication helped a candidate's image of maturity. Wit worked as well as the steroids. Kennedy would laugh away his youth by relating an anecdote from his first term in the Senate:

I was participating in a floor debate and that caused me to move closer to the front from my seat in the back row. I found myself sitting next to Senate "Dean" Carl Hayden who had entered the Congress forty years before. I asked Hayden what changes had occurred in that time and he said, "In those days new members didn't speak."

Kennedy's youth and boyish appearance became a serious liability during the nominating process. Speaker of the House Sam Rayburn was among the party leaders who were sniping at Kennedy's tender years. JFK turned the issue aside with a laugh: "Sam Rayburn may think I'm young, but then most of the population looks young to a man who's seventy-eight."

But the issue refused to go away. Harry Truman challenged Kennedy's youth before a national audience. "We need a man with the greatest possible maturity," said the former President. Kennedy attacked the argument with logic and wit. He said that if age had been a criterion, and America excluded all those under forty-four from positions of trust, such an exclusion

would have kept Jefferson from writing the Declaration of Independence, Washington from commanding the Continental

Army, Madison from fathering the Constitution, and Columbus from discovering America.

Ted Sorensen, whose graceful hand could be seen in the speech, observed afterward: "Kennedy wisely struck out the one other name I had on the list—Jesus of Nazareth."

During the campaign, Kennedy used humor to defuse the emotional issues of wealth, youth, and religion, but once he reached the White House, he found that humor was needed to defuse a very unpopular appointment.

Kennedy's father had urged him to ensconce his brother Bobby in the Cabinet so that Jack could depend on his sound advice and absolute loyalty. But when JFK made the appointment, it created a firestorm of public protest. Charges of nepotism and inexperience were heard in and out of Congress. Once again here was an issue that would not respond to cool, analytical debate. Kennedy resorted to wit and succeeded in laughing the issue out of popular discourse. Said the President of his brother's appointment as attorney general: "I see nothing wrong with giving him a little legal experience before he goes into private practice."

He disarmed members of the press by telling them how he had announced this controversial appointment: "At four in the morning, I stuck my head out the front door, looked both ways, and whispered, 'It's Bobby!' "

Jack Kennedy used humor to demonstrate his intellectual credentials and his kinship with men of ideas. The Kennedy White House had become a gathering spot for intellectuals, and public relations made the most of it. "It's become a sort of eating place for artists," laughed Kennedy. "But *they* never ask *us* out."

In point of fact, Kennedy had little taste for philosophical discussions and tortuous introspection. But he was adept at using humor to identify himself with intellectuals.

On one occasion he held a dinner honoring American Nobel Prize winners and declared:

This is the most extraordinary collection of talent that has ever been gathered together at the White House—with the possible exception of when Thomas Jefferson dined alone.

It was his way of reminding the brilliant assemblage of the creative and the cultivated that not all politicians were horny-handed hacks.

On the campaign trail, Kennedy would sprinkle his speeches with quotations from authors and poets. Sometimes his wit would distort the poetry, as when he ended a campaign speech with these familiar lines from Robert Frost:

"But I have promises to keep,
And miles to go before I sleep,
And miles to go before I sleep."
And now I go to Brooklyn.

Chapter 28
Seducing the Press

"President Kennedy is the real master of the game. He disarms you with a smile and a wise-crack."

JAMES RESTON

In the years that the Kennedy legend has been growing, the public has been subjected to tales of philandering that must be looked on with a skeptical eye. Had Kennedy bedded all the women who assert claims to such intimacy, he would have had little time for affairs of state.

But if Kennedy is guiltless of these multiple sexual seductions, he is less innocent of an ongoing seduction of the press. His chief weapon in this calculated seduction was the famous Kennedy wit.

When he was campaigning across the country in the family plane, Kennedy's conversations with reporters were always casual, ripe with banter and wisecracks. Predictably, the candidate's ironic wit endeared him to the press, which prizes humor above emeralds. This humor bonded candidate and press during the long days of the campaign and throughout the thousand days of Kennedy's truncated administration. In retrospect, many journalists feel that the adulation engendered by JFK's wit and charm prevented them from being wholly objective in the performance of their reportorial duties. Jody Powell is bitter in indicting the White House press corps for its love affair with the Kennedys, and its coolness to his own patron.

From the beginning, Jack Kennedy sensed that his success as a candidate and as a president would depend on his ability to have the media judge him in the most favorable light. He was particularly adept at courting the press during the 1960 campaign. To the extent that a seduction was afoot, what Theodore White called *The Making of the President* was really "The Making of the Press."

As a former reporter himself, Jack Kennedy was familiar with the journalists' working habits. He knew the pressures under which they worked, and understood how he could make their jobs more interesting by bringing a leavening of wit to their exchanges. Though his own daily schedule was hectic and lengthy, he would always find time to make himself available to the press. Reporters found these colloquys with Kennedy the most delightful part of the job—the parried questions, the flashing wit, the ironic asides. Said one reporter who had alternated between the Kennedy and Nixon campaigns, "Traveling with Nixon was a chore, but traveling with Kennedy was fun!" Said Laura Berquest of *Look* magazine, "I know of no newsman who covered Kennedy's campaign who didn't come away thinking he *knew* John F. Kennedy—they were no longer the press corps, but his friends." On the final day of the Kennedy campaign, columnist Mary McGrory broke into tears. "This is the end of it," she said. Kennedy put his arm around her. "We'll always be together, Mary," he smiled. One *New York Times* reporter gushed that it was as though "one of us" had made it to the Oval Office.

Whether all the feelings of friendship and camaraderie with Kennedy were reciprocal is open to question. As his roommate at Choate and Harvard, Lem Billings, told me, "I don't know if I was *his* best friend, but he was *mine*." The same might be said for the members of the press.

Reporters tend to place a high valuation on humor. It is a quality that most good reporters possess and they value it in others. To most newsmen, an intelligent wit suggests other crucial qualities, and Kennedy understood this linkage. As Hugh Sidey said, "Humor in a president goes deeper than just good gag lines. It really comes out of an intelligence and understanding of politics and a grander idea of what is the human scheme." Most journalists, bathed by the Kennedy wit, attributed this depth of understanding to JFK.

If Kennedy had assiduously courted the press during the campaign, the process accelerated once he reached the White House. He realized that the people to invite to dinner were not the publishers who sold the advertising, but the reporters who sold the public. Kennedy often chatted with a reporter under the lens of a wire service photographer. "Kennedy swept us into a world we'd never seen before," recalled Hugh Sidey. "Suddenly here you were at Hickory Hill with 'the beautiful people' you'd read about. You were on the *Honey Fitz*, or taking a nude swim with the President of the United States. . . . Kennedy brought us onto the magic carpet with him."

Jack Kennedy was careful to maintain the closest contacts with the press after he entered the White House. His narrow margin of victory emphasized the need to create the image of a witty, brilliant president, and that required the affection of the media.

In his continuing courtship of the press, Kennedy concentrated on the more influential periodicals and wire services. Representatives of the Associated Press, United Press International, *Time*, *Newsweek*, *The New York Times*, and *The Washington Post* enjoyed special attention and often found themselves the witnesses or the objects of Kennedy's ironic wit.

Merriman "Smitty" Smith, the chief correspondent for UPI, was one of those who was targeted for the Kennedy charm. Smitty's syndicated column appeared in many hundreds of newspapers around the country, and, combined with his books, lectures, and appearances on *The Jack Paar Show*, gave him a wide public influence. Kennedy wasted no time in flattering Smitty with the Kennedy wit. At a party for newsmen held a few days after the inauguration, President Kennedy seized Smitty's arm, hustled him over to the First Lady, and said, "Jackie, I want you to meet Merriman Smith. We inherited him with the White House."

Addressing a correspondents' dinner a few months later, Kennedy paid further homage to the dean of the press corps. Said the President:

> I have had during my first five months in office the close observation of Mr. Merriman Smith, who carried other presidents through difficult periods before, and who is regarded as one of the leading presidential collectors of our time.

The influence of *The New York Times* could not be ignored. Recalling that he had received the endorsement of the traditionally Republican newspaper in the campaign against Nixon, JFK tried to cement this relationship. Shortly after the election, he declared, "I am one person who can truthfully say, 'I got my job through *The New York Times*.'"

When Kennedy learned that Arthur Hays Sulzberger, chairman of the board of the *Times*, had acquired a rocking chair, he scribbled a note to him saying, "You will recall what has been said about the rocking chair—it gives you a sense of motion without any sense of danger."

Kennedy often wrote wittily to columnists, who were as flattered as they were amused. One day he received a letter from columnist Leonard Lyons, who reported that the current prices for signed photos of presidents included: George Washington, $175; Franklin D. Roosevelt, $75; U. S. Grant, $55; John F. Kennedy, $65. Kennedy wrote Lyons:

> Dear Leonard:
> I appreciate your letter about the market on Kennedy signatures. It is hard to believe that the going price is so high now. In order not to depress the market any further, I will not sign this letter.

Kennedy seldom used this kind of ingratiation on the broadcast media. While recognizing the power of TV, he felt, quite correctly, that he could best use the small screen through the televised press conferences that he employed to address the public. The TV camera effectively eliminated the broadcaster as a needless middleman. The live press conferences were held in the cavernous State Department auditorium, with Kennedy standing behind a podium and the eager press corps spread out before him like an audience for *The Tonight Show*.

The arrangement prompted Peter Lisagor of *The Chicago Daily News* to comment that reporters had become "spearcarriers in a great televised special. We were props in a show, in a performance. Kennedy mastered the art of this performance early, and I always felt that we should have joined Actors Equity." Of course, the starring performance was Kennedy's and it was a riveting one indeed.

JFK's extemporaneous wit had a marvelous showcase in these press conferences. His spontaneity did more than show his lack of pretension, it showed his agile mind as well.

Ted Sorensen has recalled that the President often had to inhibit his penchant for audacious wit. "He told me," said Sorensen, "that he had to restrain himself. He was often tempted to make some humorous remark, but he was afraid that in cold print it wouldn't look very statesmanlike."

When reporters protested the live press conferences and their own exploitation in these televised happenings, Kennedy laughed away their objections. He reassured the press, with a twist of friendly sarcasm:

> I find it highly beneficial to have some twenty million Americans regularly observe the incisive, the intelligent and the courteous qualities displayed by our Washington correspondents.

In preparing for these press conferences, Kennedy's aides compiled lists of possible queries, and then in discussing them with the President they would often come up with humorous answers for Kennedy to use. These responses were generally too caustic to use, but Sorensen recalls Kennedy weighing these barbed replies when the question turned up on camera. Reflected JFK, "It is dangerous to have them in the back of my head." He worried aloud before one press conference that it might turn into *The Six O'clock Comedy Hour.*

If James Reston called the press conferences "the goofiest idea since the hula hoop," *The Kennedy Special,* as some critics called it, was the hottest ticket in town. Both press and public were beguiled by a president who had the wit to keep his footing. Here was an early exchange:

REPORTER. The Republican National Committee recently adopted a resolution saying you were pretty much of a failure. How do you feel about that?

PRESIDENT KENNEDY. I assume it passed unanimously.

Early in his administration, questions revolved around Kennedy's choice of a Cabinet and produced this exchange:

REPORTER. Mr. President, have you narrowed your search for a new Postmaster General? Are you seeking a man with a business background or a political background?

PRESIDENT KENNEDY. The search is narrowing, but there are other fields that are still to be considered, including even a postal background.

Kennedy's antic responses could be both spontaneous and fitting:

REPORTER. There's a feeling in some quarters, sir, that big business is forcing you to come to terms. Businessmen seem to have the attitude, "Now we have you where we want you."

PRESIDENT KENNEDY. I can't believe I'm where big business wants me.

Even before he reached the White House, the Kennedy wit crackled in the give-and-take along the campaign trail:

221

REPORTER. Senator, Governor Brown today issued a very optimistic statement about your chances. Yet the field poll shows Nixon running ahead. Which of these two experts do you believe?

SENATOR KENNEDY. I believe Governor Brown.

QUESTION. I am eleven years old. What is my future with Kennedy?

SENATOR KENNEDY. Well, I am afraid that if things work out well, by the time you are twenty-one I will be finished with my second term. . . .

QUESTION. [from a small boy] Senator Kennedy, how did you become a war hero?

SENATOR KENNEDY. It was involuntary. They sank my boat.

QUESTION. I am for Kennedy. And may I visit you when you are the President of the United States in the White House? I have tried three times and cannot get in.

SENATOR KENNEDY. Let's meet outside and we'll get it all set.

Kennedy was able to laugh at some of the most crucial issues of the campaign, which endeared him to his journalistic fans:

REPORTER. President Eisenhower has been a pretty popular president. How much of a factor do you expect him to be in this campaign?

SENATOR KENNEDY. Well, I would be glad to have his cooperation but I think he is already committed.

REPORTER. Senator, you were promised a military intelligence briefing from the President. Have you received that?

SENATOR KENNEDY. Yes, I talked on Thursday to General Wheeler from the Defense Department.

REPORTER. What was his first name?

SENATOR KENNEDY. He didn't brief me on that.

REPORTER. Do you think you will lose any votes because of your Catholic religion?

SENATOR KENNEDY. I feel as a Catholic that I'll get my reward in my life hereafter, although I may not get it here.

REPORTER. Do you plan on taking your rocking chair with you to the White House if you are elected President?

SENATOR KENNEDY. Whither I goest—it goes.

Kennedy's spontaneous humor was generally sharper and more felicitous than any that had been crafted for him. He bridled at the observation by James Reston that a good deal of his "extemporaneous humor" was being ghostwritten for him, though it was known by the press that Joseph Kraft and John Bartlow Martin were preparing humor for each stop on the campaign trail.

The Kennedy wit could lash offending members of the press as quickly as it could stroke them. He was particularly sensitive to the reproaches of Arthur Krock, which led him to remark, referring to friendly columnist Doris Fleeson, "I'd rather be Fleesonized than Krocked."

When Krock criticized the President for not welcoming Katanga President Moise Tshombe to the United States, Kennedy referred to a segregated Washington club to which Krock belonged. Snapped Kennedy, "Arthur, I'll make a deal with you—I'll invite Tshombe to the United States if you'll invite him to the Metropolitan Club."

When he felt the press was not treating him fairly, Kennedy's humor could mask a threat. When a *Look* magazine reporter asked a question about an offensive rumor then in circulation, Kennedy replied, "You print that story and I just might wind up owning *Look* magazine."

But Kennedy's wit was generally free of malice. Any negative notes were more ironic than vicious. An example was embodied in this exchange which took place shortly after the start of the 1960 campaign. Vice-President Nixon had to go into the hospital and Senator Kennedy was asked about the situation this produced:

REPORTER. Senator, did you say you were not going to discuss the Vice-President until he is out of the hospital?

SENATOR KENNEDY. That's right.

REPORTER. Does that mean no personal references in your speeches?

SENATOR KENNEDY. That's right.

REPORTER. You are not going to mention him?

SENATOR KENNEDY. Unless I can praise him.

REPORTER. Do you mean as long as he stays in the hospital he has sanctuary?

SENATOR KENNEDY. Yes, that's right. I may go there.

A few days later, when Nixon remained bedridden in the hospital, the press pursued the subject:

REPORTER. Senator, when does the moratorium end on Nixon's hospitalization and your ability to attack him?

SENATOR KENNEDY. Well, I said I would not mention him unless I could praise him until he got out of the hospital, and I have not mentioned him.

There was an interesting ambivalence in Kennedy's attitude toward the press. Reporters were his friends and publishers were his foes. And thus, humor could go just so far in winning newspapers to his support.

Kennedy was too proud to act on the advice offered him by President Eisenhower, not to read the newspapers. I well recall his brother Bob tossing down a copy of a New York City paper that had rankled him, and growling, "Thank God I don't read the papers." Said JFK to one press conference, parodying a cigarette slogan of the time, "I am reading more and enjoying it less."

Kennedy was able to turn a gentle mockery toward the publications that attacked him most often. He was an addict of *Time* and *Newsweek*, but asked his opinion of *U.S. News & World Report* he replied, "I find it has little news and less to report."

But President Kennedy had no illusions of the power and ultimate independence of the press. He was fond of quoting Oscar Wilde's trenchant epigram on the subject: "In America the President reigns for four years, but Journalism governs forever."

Chapter 29
The Gridiron Dinners

"I'm glad to see my old friend Arthur Krock here. Mr. Krock has been to every major dinner in history—except the Last Supper—and he had a relative at that one."
JOHN F. KENNEDY

Each year the cream of Washington journalism celebrates its own importance at the Gridiron Club. It is an evening of off-the-record sketches and songs, pointedly humorous, and it is attended by editors, publishers, bureaucrats, lobbyists, and legislators. The influential correspondents tend to dominate the proceedings and draw up the guest list, and their invitations are not easily ignored by the President and his staff.

One of these dinners was a memorable launching pad for the Kennedy wit, and the occasion showed the young senator and his aides just how valuable humor could be to the Kennedy ambitions.

"It began," Ted Sorensen told me, "when Kennedy was invited to give the Gridiron address. He was to be the Democratic speaker for the Gridiron and he accepted. For weeks he worried more about that than anything else in the office, in the nation, in the campaign, in the world! He regretted ever having accepted it. He was hearing stories about Gridiron speakers who had fallen flat in their attempts to be funny. He was certain that if it were a success nobody would really care except to write him off as just another funny fellow. But if he were a *failure*, it would have an extremely adverse effect. . . .

He was collecting funny lines for a very long time. The speech, I'm happy to report, was a success."

Washington correspondents fill the spring season with dinners that the President and other politicians are invited to address. Some presidents, like Lyndon Johnson, have lacked the stomach for these witty confrontations and have chosen not to attend. Others like Kennedy have attended them all and created a valuable rapport with the press.

The most famous of these spring events is the Gridiron Club Dinner. Other annual banquets where presidents are summoned to entertain the lords of the press are the Alfalfa Club affair and the White House Correspondents Dinner. On these occasions Jack Kennedy was able to display not only his elegant wit but also his alert mind. At one of these dinners, as comedian Joey Bishop was addressing the guests, Kennedy was busily scribbling on the back of his menu. When he finally approached the microphone, he said, "I must ask that my remarks be kept off the record. I can't have it known that I've been entertaining a Jewish Bishop."

The 1958 Gridiron was the first to be addressed by Jack Kennedy and the one that caused him such anxiety. These affairs begin with the press needling the guest speakers in sketch and song, and then the politicians respond with their monologues. Kennedy was a major presidential candidate at the time, and the press directed an effective shaft at his father's money with a parody of Cole Porter's "My Heart Belongs to Daddy." The lyric was altered to say, "The bill belongs to daddy,/'Cause my daddy he pays it so well."

Kennedy's speech was notable for its wit and relevance. His staff had served him well. JFK would make other memorable Gridiron speeches in the future, but this first one fueled his taste for monologic humor.

Repaying the Gridiron Club members for their jabs, Kennedy said that he understood their files had recently been ransacked and that someone had stolen "your officers' election results for the next six years."

Kennedy was not alone in seeking the Democratic presiden-

227

tial nomination and he used the Gridiron microphone as a platform to mock his opponents, especially the thin-skinned Lyndon Johnson. Said Kennedy:

> I had a dream the other night, and I told Stuart Symington and Lyndon Johnson about it in the cloakroom yesterday. I told them how the Lord came into my bedroom, anointed my head, and said, "John Kennedy, I hereby appoint you President of the United States." Stu Symington said, "That's strange, Jack, because I had a similar dream last night, in which the Lord anointed me and declared *me* President of the United States." And Lyndon Johnson said, "That's very interesting, gentlemen, because I had a similar dream last night—and I don't remember anointing either one of you."

The Democratic party had a wealth of candidates, many of them in the Senate, and Kennedy reported on a poll in which they had "asked each senator about his preference for the presidency—and ninety-six senators each received one vote."

In addition to a plethora of candidates, the party was plagued by its usual internal battles. Kennedy lamented that the Democratic party was "split right down the middle—and that gives us more unity than we've had in twenty years."

Kennedy's wit turned caustic as he joked about the man who would become his opponent two years hence. Referring to Richard Nixon's transition from acrimony to sanctimony, he remarked:

> Some people used to say that Mr. Nixon was doing the basement work over at Republican Headquarters. But now they've given those janitorial duties to Sherman Adams, and moved Dick upstairs to teach the men's Bible class.

Addressing himself to the current recession and Ike's obfuscations, Kennedy said:

> As I interpret the President, we're now at the end of the beginning of the upturn of the downturn. Every bright spot the

White House finds in the economy is like the policeman bend-
ing over the body in the alley who says cheerfully, "Two of his
wounds are fatal—but the other one's not so bad."

A scant two months after taking the oath of office, Jack
Kennedy returned to the Gridiron Club, this time as the President. Richard Nixon had gone into eclipse after losing the
presidency to a virtual unknown. Kennedy showed that his
humor could scratch as well as tickle:

> I resolved long ago [he said] that if I ever reached national of-
> fice I would always go to these dinners with the leading mem-
> bers of the press. After all, Dick Nixon came to the Gridiron
> every year and look what it did for him.

Kennedy was not above needling Lyndon Johnson on his
aspirations for the presidency and his preoccupation with
Kennedy's health. Said JFK, "I did object to dedicating a
song to the White House physician, 'The Eyes of Texas Are
Upon You.' "

Kennedy used humor on the prickly subject of his appointment of a brother as attorney general and a brother-in-law as
head of the Peace Corps. Said the President:

> How could anyone accuse me of recklessly spending the tax-
> payer's money? At least, I'm doing my best to keep it all in the
> family.... And speaking of jobs for relatives, Master Robert
> Kennedy, Jr., age seven, came to see me today. But I told him
> we already had an Attorney General.

Kennedy embarked on a comedic *tour de force* on his new
Cabinet:

> Because you've all been so good to me tonight, I'm going to
> entrust in you confidential information about the real inside
> story of government—cabinet meetings. Here are the official
> minutes of what took place at the last cabinet meeting.

—The Attorney General was late again. Ever since Jimmy Hoffa organized the taxicab drivers . . .

—The Secretary of Defense had us all playing a new game on the panel by my desk—"button, button, who'll push which button." One brings in my secretary; one summons the head waiter; and the other blows up Siberia.

—The Secretary of the Treasury reported that the worst of the recession was not yet spent—but everything else was.

—The Secretary of Health, Education & Welfare said we would go ahead on grants to public schools, and the parochial schools could get a long-term loan from my father.

—I asked my Republican holdover [Douglas Dillon] what he thought was the biggest difference between President Eisenhower and myself. He said about a seven handicap.

—I told Abe Ribicoff to push the College Scholarship Bill hard. I'll need *something* to do in eight years.

It is interesting to note that Kennedy's bomb-dropping joke caused none of the stir of a similar Ronald Reagan joke twenty-four years later. Perhaps it was the times, perhaps the teller.

Jack Kennedy returned to the Gridiron Club six months after the most wrenching hours of his presidency, the Cuban missile crisis. Aides squirmed as he began his remarks with a parody of the famous speech he had made in the midst of the Cuban crisis. Said JFK:

I have tonight a very grave announcement. The Soviet Union has once again recklessly embarked upon a provocative and extraordinary change in the status quo in an area which they know full well I regard as having a special and historic relationship. I refer to the deliberate and sudden deployment of Mr. Khrushchev's son-in-law to the Vatican.

Two years before, Kennedy had parodied the stirring words of his Inaugural Address in mocking the size of the Democratic party debt. Aides felt the words were sacrosanct, but Kennedy's attitude was that of the classic Lombard comedy, *Nothing Sacred*. Said he:

We observe today not a celebration of freedom but a victory of Party, for we have sworn to pay off the same party debt our forebears ran up nearly a year and three months ago. Our deficit will not be paid off in the next hundred days, nor will it be paid off in the first one thousand days, nor in the life of this Administration. Nor, perhaps even in our lifetime on this planet. But let us begin!

Continuing his remarks to that memorable 1963 Gridiron Dinner, Kennedy returned to the subject of his Catholicism:

Speaking of the religious issue, I asked the Chief Justice whether he thought our new educational bill was constitutional. He said it was clearly constitutional—it hasn't got a prayer.

Lending a hand to the dairy farmers, Kennedy had issued a proclamation asking the public to drink more milk. He had to set the example, he said, and ribbed the assembled reporters on their own tastes in drink. Said Kennedy:

I am certainly enjoying being with you newsmen this evening. None of you know how tough it is to have to drink milk three times a day.

Kennedy singled out one newsperson for special treatment. He had been irked by some of the questions of newshen Sarah McClendon at press conferences. With Jacqueline on a state visit to India, JFK said:

I saw my wife's picture watching a snake charmer in India. As soon as I learn Sarah McClendon's favorite tune, I'm going to play it.

On this occasion, President Kennedy was accompanied to the Gridiron by his brother Ted. "I have brought my brother Teddy along this evening," he said. "We couldn't find anyone to leave him with." Teddy was running for nomination to the U.S. Senate from Massachusetts. President Kennedy swore that Teddy wasn't getting any help from home. "We're not sending in any troops, just a few training missions." He was lampooning our military missions to Southeast Asia, a subject that would soon lose much of its humorous appeal.

No president enjoyed the Gridiron dinners as much as Jack Kennedy, and none made such a spirited contribution to their gaiety. The attacks on him and his staff didn't seem to rankle—so long as they were funny and fitting. Indeed, some of the most delicious wit disparaging Jack Kennedy was spoken by Jack Kennedy. The shining moments that middle-aging New Frontiersmen recall most vividly include Kennedy's appearances at the Gridiron Club.

The 1963 appearance was to be Kennedy's last. On November 23 he was dead, and the dinner scheduled for four weeks later, at which the buoyant Kennedy wit would have sparkled again, was canceled.

Chapter 30
The Speechwriters

"Jack Kennedy was his own best speechwriter
when he had the time. Sorensen and those fellows—they were great researchers, you know."
DAVE POWERS

Every president demands a fierce loyalty from his closest aides
and speechwriters, but the ferocity of the Kennedy loyalists
makes that of others seem pale indeed.

Most of the men and women who created humor and rhetoric for our recent presidents are ready to acknowledge the role
they played in putting persuasive prose and sparkling wit into
the mouths of their patrons. But the Kennedy wordsmiths
protest too much that all of Camelot's oratory and wit were
the product of Jack Kennedy himself.

When Drew Pearson suggested that Ted Sorensen had
written much of *Profiles in Courage*, the Kennedy family demanded and received a retraction.

Whenever Sorensen is asked if he wrote the famous line
"Ask not what your country can do for you," his reply is a
wary "Ask not."

I recall passing Sorensen in the West Wing of the White
House shortly after the publication of *The Quotable Mr. Kennedy*, the book in which I excerpted some of the rhetoric and
wit from Kennedy speeches. When I praised his speeches,
Sorensen frowned and said, "No, no, those were all written by
the President."

☆ JOHN F. KENNEDY ☆

Discussing the work of Kennedy's speechwriters, JFK's friend Dave Powers, presently the curator of the Kennedy Museum, was insistent that Kennedy's speeches and humor were all his own. His writers were "great researchers."

Actually, it would be a most inappropriate use of taxpayers' money were our chief executive to spend the necessary time to write all his own pronouncements. It has been judged that Ronald Reagan spends more time than any previous president in preparing his own well-tooled speeches, yet no one would seriously suggest that he writes them all himself, or creates all his own anecdotes and one-liners.

Pressed on the point, Sorensen acknowledges that Kennedy's humor was the product of many minds, but it is not a subject on which he cares to dwell.

When Horace Busby, one of Lyndon Johnson's suppliers of humor, referred me to Joseph Kraft and John Bartlow Martin as the creators of humor for JFK on the campaign trail, and praised the efficient operation they had developed for the crafting of humor suited to each of Kennedy's whistle-stops, I spoke to Kraft, who had become a widely syndicated Washington columnist. "I don't want to seem to be ducking the question," he said, ducking the question, "but I think you'd better talk to Ted Sorensen about this." (Joseph Kraft has since gone to his reward. He is best remembered for the brilliance of his columns; few know of his felicitous contributions to the Kennedy campaign humor.)

To a great extent, Kennedy's speeches and Kennedy's wit were in style and substance the speeches and wit of Ted Sorensen. Though JFK never blindly accepted a Sorensen text and would discuss its approach and refine its content, the soaring rhetoric and sparkling wit that the public came to associate with Kennedy were Sorensen's creation.

As I said to Ted Sorensen, now an attorney practicing international business law at a prestigious Manhattan law firm, "Those who miss Jack Kennedy so dearly should bear in mind that the best of Kennedy—his eloquence and humor—are still very much alive in a law office on Park Avenue."

The Kennedy style of wit—which was a Kennedy/Sorensen style—always had a certain understated quality. It is said that good taste is the absence of exaggeration, and there was a conscious note of subtlety to the Kennedy humor. Not for Jack Kennedy was the anecdote, so favored by Lyndon Johnson and Ronald Reagan. In researching material for a one-man play called *The Kennedy Wit*, I found but one case of JFK telling a "joke" as such. It seems oddly out of place on his lips, like Bobby Kennedy making small talk.

> I went up to New York stressing physical fitness [said JFK] and in line with that [Secretary of Labor] Arthur Goldberg went over with a group to Switzerland to climb some of the mountains there. . . . When they all came back at four o'clock in the afternoon he didn't come back with them. So they sent out search parties and there was no sign that afternoon and night. The next day the Red Cross went out calling: "Goldberg, Goldberg. It's the Red Cross." Then this voice came down the mountain: "I gave at the office!"

Kennedy's humor had more of an appeal to the mind than to the funnybone. Gerald Ford resorted to puns and wordplays in his canned wit. One looks in vain for such humor in Kennedy's speeches. Lyndon Johnson had a crudity and coarseness to his humor. Not Kennedy, though Sorensen declared that on occasion Kennedy's private humor would have a bawdy streak. Kennedy would have no part of humor that was folksy—he would have groaned at the torrent of corn-fed humor that spilled from his successor, Lyndon Johnson.

Ted Sorensen recalled, in his splendid memoir-history *Kennedy*, that John Kennedy "grew tired of hearing over and over again . . . his own jokes." He was impressed by those loyal politicians who campaigned with him and at each airport and supermarket would laugh heartily at the same joke again and again.

The tasteless and the trite in humor troubled Kennedy. He used no slang or dialect in his jokes. He never found a speechwriter or humorist who was as much to his liking as

Ted Sorensen. It is difficult to accept the good once one has enjoyed the fine.

The analysis of humor is inevitably a rather sterile form of study. Suffice it to say that the Kennedy wit had a cerebral quality that was always relevant and laconic.

Kennedy rarely used humor in the body of a speech. Humor's place, for Kennedy, was at the beginning. He had a preference for historic anecdotes rather than "jokes."

"He believed," recalled Sorensen, "topical, tasteful, pertinent, pointed humor at the beginning of his remarks to be a major means of establishing audience rapport." Kennedy worked as assiduously on the witty opening of a speech as on its more serious substance.

Sorensen made a habit of scribbling down amusing lines from a toastmaster or politician for Kennedy's future use. He would jot down witty observations from newspaper columnists and the works of Will Rogers and other classic wits.

Sorensen assembled a bulging folder as his collection of pertinent humor grew. It was his practice to omit all humor from the texts of speeches that were distributed to the press. By this strategy, the jokes did not find their way into published stories and hence could be used again and again.

As Kennedy was waiting to be introduced, he could often be observed scribbling in the margin of his speech. He was consulting a typewritten humor list of one-line memory joggers and writing the opening witticism that seemed most fitting for a particular audience.

Said Sorensen of Kennedy's taste in jokes, "He liked humor that was both topical and original, irreverent but gentle." Though he was often far from gentle in his satiric thrusts at Nixon on the campaign trail, his humor was more often, in Sorensen's phrase, "subtle and self-belittling [which was] consistent with his own personality and private wit."

Lest it be assumed that Ted Sorensen's wit and rhetoric could be applied with equal felicity to another candidate, it should be noted that as co–campaign manager for presidential aspirant Gary Hart, Sorensen wrote speeches and humor for Hart, who was aping Jack Kennedy in haircut and mannerisms as well. It became apparent that Sorensen's wit and rhetoric needed a sympathetic instrument, and Gary Hart was no John F. Kennedy.

Sorensen's criterion for humor was comprehension and irony. He used short, pointed lines that exploded in unexpected wit, like Shavian epigrams. The test of a Sorensen humorous line was not how it appeared in print in next week's *Time*, but how it sounded to the ear and how it tickled the mind.

Both Sorensen and Kennedy disliked prolixity. Comedy was crisp and lean. Kennedy wanted both his witticisms and his message to be as unpretentious as the man himself. Not for JFK was the long, rambling story. The Kennedy wit was marked by a brevity that made the lines remembered and repeated.

Here are a few examples that demonstrate the concision and thrust of the Kennedy wit:

I recognize that in the last campaign most of the members of the N.A.M. supported my opponent, except for a very few who were under the impression that I was my father's son.

There is no city in the United States in which I get a warmer welcome and less votes than Columbus, Ohio.

After some debate and protest, it was decided that I would not make this speech in Spanish.

Mr. Nixon has had his troubles in this campaign. At one point even the Wall Street Journal was criticizing his tactics. That is like the Osservatore Romano criticizing the Pope.

Senator McNamara is my seatmate in the Senate—between the two of us we usually vote right.

Washington is a wonderful city—it's a blend of northern charm and southern efficiency.

I want to express my regrets for being late. They told me five
days ago a storm was coming up here, so we waited.

A combination of loyalty and discretion has led Ted Sorensen to diminish the role he played in the Kennedy rhetoric
and the Kennedy humor. A similar attitude silenced another
supplier of the Kennedy wit, political satirist Mort Sahl.

He reluctantly acknowledged his own comic contributions
to the Kennedy cause.

"Yes, I was juicing up the speeches," Sahl told me. "The
old man got ahold of me—the ambassador—and asked me to
work for Jack. Sorensen and Salinger used to deliver it to
Kennedy on the plane, because I was all over the place at the
college concerts. I felt that it would best serve him if it was un-
dercover. In other words, my opinion would be if an actor told
me he was working for a candidate, I would vote for his opponent."

Sahl expressed a special affection for the humor of presidents. "I use a lot of presidential humor verbatim in my act
now," he said. "To great effect."

Sahl has little regard for contemporary comedians and feels
that certain public figures are funnier by far.

"It only reaffirms what I felt from the beginning," said
Sahl. "The comedians are the last ones to know. The real
humor comes from someone with a sense of urban irony ...
you know, like Gene McCarthy. It never comes from the guy
we *pay* to hear do it."

Reflecting on the humor he supplied to John F. Kennedy,
Mort Sahl laughed his explosive laugh that has become familiar to a generation of educated audiences.

"Jack Kennedy needed less help with humor than anybody
alive!"

Chapter 31
A Sense of
Security

"I know who I am and I don't have to worry
about adapting and changing. All I have to do
. . . is be myself."
JOHN F. KENNEDY

Observers of the Washington scene sometimes ponder the absence of humor in a Richard Nixon and its abundance in a John F. Kennedy, and come away from the problem persuaded that it is a matter of a sense of security.

Kennedy's humor was not primarily the product of imported gagwriters and perspiring speechwriters, with one eye on the headlines and the other on the President's schedule. It was a product of the Kennedy self-confidence.

John Kennedy's humor, like his hubris, grew from his courage and character. While he would always share the presidential malady of sensitivity to criticism, the carping of foes could never dislodge the solid foundation of the Kennedy confidence.

Lewis J. Paper, in his incisive work *The Promise and the Performance: The Leadership of John F. Kennedy*, focuses on the source and the quality of the Kennedy character. He points out that at those moments when he was most sorely tested—in Berlin and Cuba and the Solomon Islands—Kennedy was calm, courageous, cocky, and wisecracking. Joseph P. Kennedy's not inconsiderable wealth had insulated Jack from the customary crises of youth, and the young JFK felt little obligation to take life very seriously. His carefree attitude was reflected in the quick wit that showed itself in and out of school. It was the same wit—somewhat refined and matured—that would enliven press conferences, remarks in the Rose Garden, speeches to the Gridiron Club, and forays on the campaign trail. It made its first appearance while Jack Kennedy was still a student at Choate, the tony prep school where he spent his early formative years.

David Horowitz and Peter Collier's mordant biography, *The Kennedys*, reveals occasional flashes of the young Kennedy's sense of humor. With roommate Lem Billings as his hapless target, the Kennedy wit of those early years often had a cruel element, as when he offered Billings the irresistible sum of a hundred dollars to strip naked and sing a risqué Mae West ballad to Jack's father.

George St. John, Kennedy's tutor during those Choate years, once wrote to Joseph Kennedy about Jack's audacious wit in a way that seems, in retrospect, to be especially incisive and to contain reassurance for parents troubled by their own antic offspring. Said the tutor:

> Jack has a clever, individualistic mind. . . . When he learns the right place for humor and learns to use his individual way of looking at things as an asset instead of a handicap, his natural gift of an individual outlook and witty expression are going to help him. [Indeed they did!] A more conventional mind and a more plodding and mature point of view would help him a lot more right now; but we have to allow, my dear Mr. Kennedy, with boys like Jack, for a period of adjustment. All that natural cleverness Jack has to learn how to use in his life and work. . . .

John Kennedy's undergraduate wit must have been extremely troublesome to his father to require his tutor to write so persuasively to allay the elder Kennedy's concern. Doubtless Joe Kennedy thought Jack's humor was a sign of a frivolous mind. When Joseph Kennedy launched into a dinner table tirade at his brood for their extravagances, Jack waited for the shouting to subside and then cracked, "The only solution is for dad to work harder." Jack Kennedy's tutor was prescient in assessing the value of the boy's wit and the wisdom that it augured.

When John Kennedy filed to run in the Democratic congressional primary in Massachusetts, his father's wealth was at the root of his campaign. But JFK's chief assets were his own charm and wit. They earned interest in a way that financial assets could never have done.

The center of the campaign was John Fitzgerald Kennedy and his exhilarating wit. The campaign seemed a long shot. But the indefatigable Kennedy, plagued by illness, would arise at six A.M. to shake hands with the workers at all the factories in the district.

Dave Powers later recalled those early days with pleasure. "I was with him from the beginning," said Powers. "And the two things he never lost were his humor and his humility. He was the same man on Bunker Hill in Massachusetts and on Capitol Hill and at 1600 Pennsylvania Avenue."

From early morning till late at night Kennedy and Powers knocked on doors, climbed the steep tenement steps, and attended countless tea parties. Kennedy spoke to anyone and everyone, turning on the boyish charm that came so easily, joking and joshing, using a mixture of levity and gravity.

"He had a great sense of humor," recalled Powers. "A real Irish sense of humor. I called it a three-decker sense of humor, because of the tenements where he campaigned. You know, Mrs. Sullivan would be on the first floor, Mrs. Donovan on the second, and Mrs. O'Neill on the third. In that first campaign I took him through that Boston tenement district and he learned a lot about the three-decker Irish."

He also learned how to win them with wit, a facility that would grow with the years.

241

"He'd get a great laugh out of the stories we told him about the Boston Irish," recalled Powers. "He had a Bob Hope style. There were these one- and two-liners. He could use the news of the day. They loved him. He was a grand man!"

Powers beamed. "I called him Jack for fourteen years, and the first day in the White House I walked into the Oval Office and I said, 'Good morning, Mr. President,' and he turned and looked at me and said, 'Good morning, Ambassador.' He wasn't used to having old pals call him Mr. President yet."

Jack Kennedy's wit rested primarily on his knowledge of his own abilities, his insight as to who and what he was. He seemed completely comfortable being himself. It used to be said of popular entertainers that none of them know who they are. They have no sense of identity. That's why it's such a pleasure to see Sammy Davis, Jr. He knows exactly who he is. He's Frank Sinatra.

Jack Kennedy knew precisely who he was. And this attitude was exemplified during the 1960 campaign when he was asked if he was tired. Kennedy replied in the negative and added that he was certain Nixon was exhausted. Kennedy explained:

> I know who I am and I don't have to worry about adapting and changing. All I have to do at each stop is be myself. But Nixon doesn't know who he is, and so each time he makes a speech he has to decide which Nixon he is, and that can be very exhausting.

It was in this hard-fought campaign that Kennedy's sharp wit became a potent weapon. Supplemented by the ironic barbs of alter ego Ted Sorensen and the "indigenous" jokes of Joe Kraft and John Bartlow Martin, the Kennedy wit helped the candidate deal with the most vexing issues.

And because he could be himself rather than go through chameleon exertions, there was little tension in his manner. Wit was a leavening for the public; it was also a stimulant for the candidate.

Responding to a string of Nixon epithets (which on this occasion were not deleted), Kennedy said, "Mr. Nixon, in the last seven days, has called me an ignoramus, a Pied Piper, and all the rest. I've just confined myself to calling him a Republican, but he says that is hitting below the belt." Kennedy's Choate tutor must have been smiling with satisfaction.

Sometimes a caustic quality invaded Kennedy's humor, as when he observed, "Do you realize the responsibility I carry? I'm the only person standing between Nixon and the White House." (With the assassination of John Kennedy and his younger brother, this bit of antic wit proved prophetic: With neither Kennedy now standing between Nixon and the White House, he proceeded to occupy it.)

Jack Kennedy's air of confidence made him feel at home wherever he found himself. Many politicians—like Zelig, the chameleon creation of Woody Allen—take on the coloration of whomever they are among. They wear hardhats and Indian war bonnets. They lunge at voters and shake their hands. They wave their arms and roll their eyes. Jack Kennedy did not lunge or wear funny hats. He was calmly and composedly himself, wherever he went.

That is not to say that he did not address his remarks and his wit to a particular audience. He was quite brilliant in focusing his humor and intelligence on his auditors.

To the farmers of Grandview, Missouri, he said, "How can any farmer vote Republican? I understand nearby there was a farmer who planted some corn. He said to his neighbor, 'I hope I break even this year. I really need the money.'"

To a group of the party faithful in Salt Lake City who had just paid one hundred dollars a plate for a modest dinner, he said, "I am deeply touched, but not as touched as you have been by coming to this dinner."

Kennedy's aplomb on the campaign trail was due in no small part to the talented duo who preceded him on his odyssey. Joseph Kraft and John Bartlow Martin had a very special assignment: to assemble information on each city on the candidate's schedule and prepare a bevy of relevant jokes referring to local lore. Horace Busby has recalled, "Kraft and Martin's operation was magnificent—the way they prepared jokes that were appropriate to each particular audience."

According to Ted Sorensen, Kraft and Martin worked tirelessly as "speech advance men." In addition to preparing notes on local issues for Kennedy's use in speeches at airports, railroad stations, and shopping malls, they would provide the candidate with relevant one-liners to open these brief talks.

Creating comedy that is appropriate to a particular city and situation, humor that is good-natured, felicitous, and funny, is no mean feat. In traveling through New York State with Bobby Kennedy in his quest for a seat in the U.S. Senate, and writing humor that was relevant to locales as disparate as Niagara Falls, Rochester, Albany, and Coney Island, I felt the problem keenly. Jack Kennedy was well served by Kraft and Martin.

In Pittsburgh he said:

> I'm glad to be here in Pittsburgh because I feel a sense of kinship with the Pittsburgh Pirates. Like my candidacy, they were not given much chance in the spring.

In Florida, Kennedy referred to his parents and to the nation's ailing economy:

> I come here to Florida today where my family has lived for thirty years and I feel it looks pretty good at least to get two votes in Florida.
>
> Those of you who live in Florida depend upon a moving and expanding country. I know something about the economy of this state. When the rest of the country catches cold, Florida gets pneumonia and Miami is very sick.

Kennedy counted congressmen when he arrived in the Lone Star State:

> Texas has sent twenty-one Democratic Congressmen to the Congress, and one Republican, a fair proportion, a good aver-

age. . . . There is a story about a Texan who went to New York and told a New Yorker that he could jump off the Empire State Building and live. The easterner said, "Well, that would be an accident." He said, "Suppose if I did it twice?" The easterner said, "That would be an accident too." "Suppose I did it three times?" And the easterner said, "That would be a habit." Texas twice jumped off the Democratic band wagon [to vote for Ike]. We are down here to see it is not going to be a habit.

In Nevada, a crowd waited for JFK till the early hours of the morning and he said:

I want to express my appreciation to you for your generous reception at 4:30 in the morning. Back East the Democrats go to bed at nine o'clock regardless of what happens, so I was very impressed.

In California, his opponent's home state, Kennedy combined flattery and wit in a felicitous brew:

It seems to me that the great story of California has come about because people were not satisfied with things as they were. They liked Massachusetts and they liked Ohio and they liked Oklahoma, but they thought they could do better and they came to California. . . . I don't know why they felt that way about Massachusetts.

In Alaska, Kennedy pointed out his resolution in seeking their votes:

There are three electoral votes in Alaska. I left Washington, D.C., this morning at 8 o'clock. It is now 11:30 in Washington. I have come, I figure, about 3,000 miles per electoral vote, and if I travel 800,000 miles in the next two months, we might win this election. But I am prepared to do it.

On the plains of Wyoming, Kennedy paid witty tribute to the broad horizons:

There is a story that once a traveler from Boston used to complain that the train stood still at night in the West, and the reason, of course, was that when he woke up in the morning, they saw the same mountains and the same rivers that they had seen the previous morning.

In Minnesota, Kennedy had the grace and guile to praise his former primary rival Hubert Humphrey, in his home state:

This week I had the opportunity to debate Mr. Nixon. I should reveal that I had a great advantage in that debate. Mr. Nixon had just debated with Khrushchev and I had debated with Hubert Humphrey and that gave me an edge.

In Iowa, campaigning before five hundred farmers, Kennedy said:

I come from a nonagricultural state, Massachusetts, and therefore I am sure that there are some farmers here in Iowa who say, "Why should we elect someone from New England? Why shouldn't we elect a farmer?" Well, there is no farmer up for the office this year. Whittier, California, is not one of the great agricultural sections of the United States.

In the Bronx, Kennedy stretched a point with humor to present himself as a native son:

I said up the street that I am a former resident of the Bronx. Nobody believes that, but it's true. I went to school in the Bronx. Now, Riverdale is part of the Bronx, and I lived there for six years. No other candidate for the presidency can make that statement.

Traveling to the borough of Brooklyn, Kennedy revealed another string to his bow, the humor of hyperbole:

Brooklyn was the first district to endorse me as a candidate for president. My own family had not even endorsed me when you endorsed me.

To the women of Wilmington, Delaware, he made an offer they could not refuse:

When I came to Washington to the U.S. Senate, I brought a number of young ladies from Massachusetts to be secretaries. They all got married. So if any of you girls feel the prospects are limited in this community, you come to Washington and work for me.

In San Antonio, Texas, Bostonian Kennedy told a story that was ideal in its ingratiation and locale:

They tell of a man from Boston who visited the Alamo here in San Antonio and a Texan was boasting about the courage of the men who fought here—Bowie and Crockett and the rest. And finally the Bostonian had heard enough and he said, "Haven't you ever heard of Paul Revere?" And the Texan said, "Oh yes, he's the guy who ran for help."

In whatever city he visited, Kennedy had a sufficient sense of security to laugh at the opposition and to challenge the Republicans in the crowd to declare themselves. In Ohio he said:

There is a terrible rumor to the effect that this is a Republican community. I am sure it is not true. But it would be interesting to know how many Republicans we have here today. Will you hold up your hands? Let us see how many Republicans with an open mind we have got. . . . Two . . . Well, there is some prospect.

Kennedy was even secure enough to admit his own exhaustion, a degree of candor unusual in candidates, who normally present themselves as both omniscient and omnipotent.

I personally have lived through ten presidential campaigns, but I must say the eleventh makes me feel like I lived through twenty-five.

Presidential comedy writers are quick to admonish their clients that political humor should always be genial and self-deprecating, never mean or malicious. Yet during the whirlwind campaign of 1960, the cocky, confident Kennedy did not hesitate to draw blood with mocking jokes about Richard Nixon and the Republican party.

Look at the Republicans who have run this century [he said]. Mr. McKinley, Harding—do you know what his slogan was?—"Return to Normalcy," "Keep Cool with Coolidge," "A Chicken in Every Pot" with Herbert Hoover. I don't know what Dewey's slogan was because we never really found out.

Referring to Nixon's kitchen debate with Nikita Khrushchev, Kennedy said: "Mr. Nixon may be very experienced in his kitchen debates. So are a great many other married men I know."

Referring to the Nixon slogan emphasizing experience, Kennedy cracked, "Experience is what Mr. Nixon will have left after this campaign is over."

Kennedy was quick to exploit a question asked President Eisenhower about his vice-president's decision-making powers:

A reporter asked President Eisenhower about a month ago what suggestions and ideas Nixon has had, and the President said, "Give me a week and I will let you know."

Nixon insisted that Ike was "just kidding" but the avuncular Eisenhower was not notable for his levity and so the remark was costly.

Kennedy's quiet confidence enabled him to slip a punch better than any president before or since. He used the cool humor of understatement to turn attacks back on his attackers, what the Kennedys like to call turning lemons into lemonade. When a group of hecklers continually chanted, "We want Nixon," Kennedy smiled, "I don't think you're going to get him."

Kennedy could make the humor of his attacker boomerang by simply repeating it:

> Someone was kind enough, though I don't know whether he meant it kindly, to say that I sound like a Truman with a Harvard accent.

Responding to the attacks of the Reverend Norman Vincent Peale, Kennedy commented:

> We had an interesting convention at Los Angeles and we ended with a strong Democratic platform which we called "The Rights of Man." The Republican platform has also been presented. I do not know its title, but it has been referred to as "The Power of Positive Thinking."

On another occasion Kennedy responded to Peale's opprobrium by saying:

> Last week a noted clergyman was quoted as saying that our society may survive in the event of my election but it certainly won't be what it was. I would like to think he was complimenting me, but I'm not sure he was.

Adlai Stevenson had been wittier still in responding to an attack from Norman Vincent Peale. Introduced to the Houston Baptist convention by its leader, who said, "Governor, you are here as a courtesy, because we have already been instructed to vote for your opponent by Norman Vincent Peale," Stevenson replied, "Speaking as a Christian, I would like to say that I find the Apostle Paul appealing and the Apostle Peale appalling."

Kennedy was sufficiently secure to laugh at the excesses of the Democratic party, which had gone deeply in debt in support of his candidacy.

"I have been informed," he said after his election, "that I

am now responsible as the leader of the Democratic Party for a debt of over one million dollars." He paused. "I don't know—they spent it like they were sure we were going to win."

Given the tender ego and flamboyant behavior of his running mate, Lyndon Johnson, Kennedy's own sense of security was often tested by their uneasy political marriage. It is a credit to the Kennedy cool that he could laugh at the Johnson bombast rather than resent it.

On election night of 1960, as his staff waited nervously for the returns to flow in, Kennedy phoned Johnson long distance, then hung up and gave his people the ironic Kennedy version of the conversation.

"Lyndon says he hears that *I'm* losing Ohio but *we're* doing fine in Pennsylvania."

Kennedy's sense of security was such that he was able to accept fulsome praise with grace and a sense of his own worth. On one occasion he was introduced by a colleague with what seemed excessive zeal, even for a politician. Kennedy moved to the microphone, smiled, and said:

Every time he introduces me as potentially the greatest president in the history of the United States, I always think perhaps he is overstating it by one or two degrees. George Washington wasn't a bad President, and I do want to say a word for Thomas Jefferson. But otherwise I will accept the compliment.

Chapter 32
Laughter in Camelot

"I feel any minute somebody's going to walk in and say, 'All right, you three guys, get out of here!' "

TEDDY KENNEDY

On my first visit to the White House, President Kennedy's genial secretary, Evelyn Lincoln, had directed me to come to the northeast gate. I did so and confronted a uniformed guard in a small booth. I told him that I had an appointment to see President Kennedy, and he asked to see some identification. I fished in my wallet and pulled out my Diners Club card. "That's fine," he assured me. He snapped up the phone and said, "Mr. Gardner of the Diners Club to see the President."

There is something appropriate about this kind of error being made in the Kennedy White House. There was an antic quality, an impulsive energy that permeated the West Wing during the Kennedy years. They were years of potential— much of it unrealized and illusory—and tremendous excitement.

The closing scenes of Stephen Sondheim's musical *Merrily We Roll Along* reflect some of the energy and promise of those years. For the first time the corridors of power, long occupied by staid, grandfatherly figures, rang with the footsteps, the exclamations, and the laughter of a younger generation.

Kennedy's laughter was contageous and, like most qualities in an organization, came from the top. Just as corruption is self-propagating, so is laughter. It is suggestive that John F. Kennedy's chief speechwriter was also his chief joke writer. Kennedy liked the company and stimulation of witty men and women. As Ted Sorensen told me, "He regarded a sense of humor as a highly prized quality in the people with whom he worked. Because he had an excellent sense of humor of his own, he liked to hear jokes, he liked funny lines, he liked funny remarks. He liked to speak them and hear them."

Kennedy often directed his humor at members of his staff. As Sorensen remarked, "He was pretty good at putting the needle into others."

Kennedy ribbed Clark Clifford, the Washington attorney who had helped in the transition period. Kennedy said, with awe and gratitude, that Clifford had chosen the entire Kennedy Cabinet, and had even chosen the Kennedy subcabinet. "And all he ever asked in return," said Kennedy, "was that we advertise his law firm on the back of the one-dollar bills."

When speechwriter Sorensen produced a mini-storm of protest with a speech he himself delivered in Nebraska attacking the state's educational system, Kennedy said, "That's what happens when you let a speechwriter write his own speech."

Kennedy could take an ironic attitude toward the vexations that had been passed on to him by the Eisenhower administration. At a National Security Council meeting the problems were collected within a folder. Kennedy mused, "Let's see now, did we inherit these, or are they our own?"

On the day I met him in the Oval Office, Kennedy gestured toward a puppy that was scampering across the White House lawn in the middle distance, and said, "Premier Khrushchev sent my daughter that dog. It's the offspring of the dogs the Soviets sent into orbit. I think he's trying to tell me something."

That was typical of the Kennedy wit: relevant, spontaneous, sardonic, funny.

Bob Hope, that friend and golfing partner to all presidents of recent history, later recalled his meetings with JFK.

"He always wanted to hear jokes," said Hope. "He *loved* to hear jokes."

Sometimes Kennedy preferred to hear them rather than tell them, as this episode related by Ted Sorensen reveals.

The President, Dean Rusk, McGeorge Bundy, and Sorensen were meeting on a foreign policy matter when Kennedy cryptically remarked, "He's a good dancer too." The President and Sorensen laughed but Rusk and Bundy just looked perplexed.

"That's the punchline of a funny story I was telling Ted," said the President.

"Tell it," said Bundy.

"Ted, tell them the story," said Kennedy.

Here it is as Sorensen related it to me:

A girl meets a man at a bar and after a few drinks they go back to his apartment. He tells her his name is Peterson and he's a top official at the Department of the Interior. She's very impressed and they end up in bed.

After a few subsequent meetings, the girl phones the Department of the Interior and asks to speak to Mr. Peterson.

"There's no Mr. Peterson here," she's told.

She insists that he's an important official there but no one knows of any Mr. Peterson. Finally they refer her to the Personnel Department.

"Oh yes," she is told, "we *do* have a Mr. Peterson. But he's not a top official. He's just a pheasant plucker."

"Yes," says the girl, "and he's a good dancer too."

Sometimes the Kennedy wit, playful and audacious, would infect the reporters who covered him. Merriman Smith, so seemingly solemn, once told me, "You know, Kennedy's aides are intriguing. When Arthur Schlesinger walks, he leans forward, and when McGeorge Bundy walks, he leans backward. So at the precise instant that they pass one another in the hall, they form an X."

Sorensen had his inspired moments too. During the campaign, Kennedy had hectored Nixon with the charge "I'm tired of getting up every morning and reading in the newspaper what *Khrushchev* is doing! I want to wake up and see headlines about what our *President* is doing." So one morning Sorensen burst into the President's office holding a newspaper whose front page was blanketed by Kennedy headlines. Said Sorensen, "People are tired of waking up every morning and reading what *Kennedy* is doing! They want to know what *Khrushchev* is doing."

On another occasion, when Kennedy imprudently started a fire in the Oval Office fireplace and succeeded in filling the West Wing with dense black smoke, Sorensen rushed in "to save George Washington's portrait."

Laughter is good for body and soul, as Norman Cousins has attested, and Kennedy used it to keep the tension at bay among his hardworking White House crew.

Each afternoon he would take a dip in the White House pool with Dave Powers, exchanging bawdy anecdotes with his old friend of the triple-decker tenement days.

Kennedy had a way of praising those who were closest to him with a mixture of hyperbole and whimsy that recalled the prep school Kennedy whose comic excesses had so troubled his father. Speaking of his personal secretary after calling her with an urgent summons, Kennedy said:

> Mrs. Lincoln is always sweet and unsurprised. If I had said just now, "Mrs. Lincoln, I have cut off Jackie's head, would you please send over a box?" she would have replied, "That's wonderful, Mr. President, I'll send it right away. . . . Did you get your nap?"

This kind of extravagant wit, which had so troubled his father, was having a bonding effect on the people who were so fiercely loyal to the President.

There was still something of the boy in the man. There was a sense of joy and disbelief at actually living in the White

House. Kennedy never outgrew the feeling of excitement at actually working in the Oval Office and "commuting" from the mansion upstairs. Kennedy once invited his brother Teddy and his friend Paul Fay into the Oval Office for a chat. The room was still being decorated by Mrs. Kennedy and JFK sat down in the executive swivel chair, the only chair in the virtually empty room. The President spun around in the chair, grinned mischievously, and said, "Well, Teddy, do you think it's adequate?" His brother replied, "I feel any minute somebody's going to walk in and say, 'All right, you three guys, get out of here!' "

Unlike Nixon, for whom the subject was not a humorous one, Kennedy could even joke about corruption in the White House, probably because it would find such an inhospitable climate there. Mike Feldman handled pressure groups for Kennedy. Among these were business associations for whom Feldman acted as a liaison on requests for subsidies, tariffs, and airline routes. Cracked Kennedy, "If Mike ever turns dishonest, we could all go to jail!"

Like most of us, Kennedy laughed at the things that vaguely worried him, like succession to his office through death. Planning a flight through an impending storm, he said to an aide, "If that plane goes down, Lyndon will have this place cleaned out in twenty-four hours."

The mocking humor was prophetic. Robert Kennedy was enraged that within twenty-four hours after his brother's death in Dallas, Lyndon Johnson had the Oval Office cleaned out from stem to stern and his own possessions installed.

It is often observed that Jimmy Carter was a serious president, Richard Nixon was a nervous president, and Jack Kennedy was a happy president. Quoting Aristotle, Kennedy would say that happiness is the full use of one's faculties along the lines of excellence, and the President's job offered him such employment. He seemed to relish the challenges while using his humor to better handle the pressures.

His mood was generally sanguine and joyous. Nothing could dim his sense of humor for long. The public saw it gleaming through his responses at TV press conferences. Reporters saw it at their annual farragoes such as the Gridiron Club and the White House Correspondents dinners. It was a delicious byproduct of the job. It was never manufactured to order. It was an ingredient of his character and flowed naturally down the corridors of power. It was dry, wry, ironic, and as Sorensen has acknowledged, often bawdy. "He wasn't above telling or laughing at ribald jokes that can't appear in your book," said Sorensen. His humor was a part of his perceptions, not a conscious effort to amuse, as it often becomes with other public figures. There was no "presidential pause" before a Kennedy punchline. The Kennedy wit was an integral part of the Kennedy conversation.

He kidded his staff, his wife, his brothers, his critics, his opponents, columnists, reporters, and congressmen. He said, "I do not promise to consider race or religion in my appointments. I promise only that I will not consider them." And he did not consider race, creed, color, or rank in his humor.

But most appealing of all, Kennedy liked to laugh at himself. "That ability," said Sorensen, "the ability to laugh at himself and avoid pomposity, was a quality that was central to his success in politics and in the White House." Kennedy had the grace to laugh at the trappings of power, the solemn pronouncements, the encomiums, and the attacks. As Sorensen expressed it with his usual economy, "He took his problems seriously but never himself."

Despite the excesses of legend, there can be little doubt that the luminous Kennedy wit brightened the nation during the thousand days that Jack Kennedy occupied the Oval Office.

Laughter ran round the table in the State Dining Room; it could be heard at the somber coffin-shaped table in the Cabinet Room; it flashed like lightning at his televised press conferences. Kennedy had the ability to stand as an observer to the absurdities of history. His amusement "never severed the cord of action," as Arthur Schlesinger, Jr., expressed it, but it served to illuminate problems and lighten loads. It punctured the pomposity of the proud, and was one of the vital factors in his meteoric rise to political power.

Laughter was indeed a vital part of the Kennedy legend. But as Schlesinger has observed, "Kennedy was more a realist than a romantic," and it is possible that the ironic JFK would have found humor in the idea of picturing his administration as a modern Camelot.

Revisionist scholars often use the Kennedy wit as a stick with which to beat the Kennedy legend. They point to Kennedy's humor as prime evidence of the shallowness of the Kennedy mind, as if to show that his reputation rested in wit, not wisdom; style, not substance. They concede his charm and proceed to denigrate his accomplishments.

The revisionists attack the glamour and wit, asserting that the hero of Camelot cared little about creating laws and much about creating image. His wit, they say, was designed to seduce press and public, while his achievements were of small consequence. Johnson, they conclude, lacked Kennedy's elegant wit but he knew how to exercise power and pass laws.

There is some truth in the detractors' demolitions. Man cannot live by style alone. Yet two decades after John Kennedy's death, the memory of the man is green and touched by legend. On one of my visits to Washington, I stood outside the White House and recalled my first visit and my meeting with the vigorous, youthful man who was living there.

There can be no denying that style and wit were crucial elements of the Kennedy myth. There can be no forgetting the rhetoric and humor that were so inherently a part of this cool, confident Bostonian—the humor that punctured pomp, cut through pretention, and made us laugh at our illusions.

That may be why, despite the genial wit of Ronald Reagan,

there seems to be such a want of exhilaration and such a sense of loss in Washington and in the White House. It may be why there is both humor and sadness in what Kennedy said to Arthur Schlesinger after the Bay of Pigs fiasco.

"Arthur," he said, "when you write the history of my first term—*The Only Years* . . ."

Acknowledgments

Theodore Sorensen, Dave Powers, Pierre Salinger, Arthur Schlesinger, Jr., Barry Grey, Theodore White, Evelyn Lincoln, Walter Heller, Richard Goodwin, Peter Lawford, Joseph Kraft, Hugh Sidey, James MacGregor Burns, Mort Sahl, Mark Russell, Art Buchwald, Richard Reeves, Merriman Smith, Harry Middleton, Bob Hardesty, George Reedy, Horace Busby, Douglass Cater, Harry McPherson, Frank Cormier, Ernie Cuneo, Liz Carpenter, Joe Laitin, Doris Kearns, Aram Bakshian, Bob Orben, Robert Hartmann, Milton A. Friedman, Paul Theis, David Hume Kennerly, Don Penny, James Wooten, Greg Schneiders, James Fallows, Jack Watson, Jim Lake, Lou Cannon, William Troxler, David Frost, Marc Jaffe, Susan Schwartz, Tom Wallace, Fern Weber, Phyllis Wender, Lindsay Gardner, Jason Epstein, Betty Rollin, Bill Adler, Sammy Davis, Jr., Bob Smith, Harriet Gardner, Martin Kaplan, Ross Brown, John Hersey ... the John F. Kennedy Library, the Lyndon B. Johnson Library and Museum, the Gerald R. Ford Library, the Jimmy Carter Museum ... and most especially James Landis and Jane Meara.

Bibliography

Part One:
Ronald Reagan

Barrett, Laurence I. *Gambling with History: Ronald Reagan in the White House.* Garden City, N.Y.: Doubleday, 1983.

Boyarsky, Bill. *The Rise of Ronald Reagan.* New York: Random House, 1968.

Brown, Edmund. *Reagan and Reality.* New York: Praeger, 1970.

Cannon, Lou. *Reagan.* New York: Putnam, 1982.

———. *Ronnie and Jesse.* New York: Doubleday, 1969.

Davis, Kathy Randall. *But What's He Really Like?* Menlo Park, Calif.: Pacific Coast Publishers, 1970.

Devine, Donald John. *Reagan Electionomics.* Ottawa, Ill.: Green Hill Publishers, 1983.

Drew, Elizabeth. *Campaign Journal.* New York: Macmillan, 1985.

Dugger, Ronnie. *On Reagan: The Man and His Presidency.* New York: McGraw-Hill, 1983.

Evans, Rowland, and Novak, Robert. *The Reagan Revolution.* New York: Dutton, 1981.

Gardner, Gerald. *The Actor.* New York: Pocket Books, 1981.

———. *Who's in Charge Here?* Campaign edition. New York: Ballantine Books, 1980.

Gartner, Alan, ed. *What Reagan Is Doing to Us.* New York: Harper & Row, 1982.

Germond, Jack. *Blue Smoke and Mirrors.* New York: Viking Press, 1981.

Germond, Jack, and Witcover, Jules. *Wake Us When It's Over.* New York: Macmillan, 1985.

Haig, Alexander. *Caveat.* New York: Macmillan, 1984.

Leamer, Lawrence. *Make-Believe: The Story of Nancy & Ronald Reagan.* New York: Harper & Row, 1983.

McClelland, John, ed. *Hollywood on Ronald Reagan.* Winchester, Mass.: Faber and Faber, 1983.

Perry, Roland. *Hidden Power: The Programming of the President.* New York: Beaufort Books, 1984.

Reagan, Ronald. *Public Papers of the Presidents of the U.S.,* containing the public messages, speeches, and statements of the President. Washington, D.C.: U.S. Government Printing Office, 1980–1985.

————. *The Speeches of Governor Ronald Reagan, Presidential Campaign of 1980.* Washington, D.C.: U.S. Government Printing Office, 1981.

————. *The Speeches of President Ronald Reagan, Presidential Campaign of 1984.* Washington, D.C.: U.S. Government Printing Office, 1985.

Troxler, L. William, ed. *Along Wit's Trail.* New York: Holt, Rinehart & Winston, 1983.

Valis, Wayne, ed. *The Future Under President Reagan.* Westport, Conn.: Arlington House, 1981.

Van der Linden, Frank. *The Real Reagan.* New York: Morrow, 1981.

White, F. Clifton. *Why Reagan Won.* Chicago: Regnery Gateway, 1981.

Part Two:
JIMMY CARTER

Adler, Bill, ed. *The Wit and Wisdom of Jimmy Carter.* Secaucus, N.J.: Citadel Press, 1977.

Carter, Hugh Alton. *Cousin Birdie and Cousin Hot: My Life with the Carter Family of Plains, Georgia.* Englewood Cliffs, N.J.: Prentice-Hall, 1978.

Carter, Jimmy. *A Government as Good as Its People.* New York: Simon and Schuster, 1977.

————. *Keeping Faith: Memoirs of a President.* New York: Bantam Books, 1982.

————. *Public Papers of the Presidents of the U.S.,* containing the public messages, speeches, and statements of the President. Washington, D.C.: U.S. Government Printing Office, 1977–1980.

————. *The Speeches of Governor Jimmy Carter, Presidential Campaign of 1976*. Washington, D.C.: U.S. Government Printing Office, 1977.

————. *The Speeches of President Jimmy Carter, Presidential Campaign of 1980*. Washington, D.C.: U.S. Government Printing Office, 1981.

Johnson, Haynes. *In the Absence of Power*. New York: Viking Press, 1980.

Jordan, Hamilton. *Crisis: The Last Year of the Carter Presidency*. New York: Putnam, 1982.

Kucharsky, David. *The Man from Plains: The Mind and Spirit of Jimmy Carter*. New York: Harper & Row, 1976.

Lasky, Victor. *Jimmy Carter: The Man and the Myth*. New York: R. Marek, 1979.

Mollenhoff, Clark. *The President Who Failed: Carter Out of Control*. New York: Macmillan, 1980.

Powell, Jody. *The Other Side of the Story*. New York: Morrow, 1984.

Schram, Martin. *Running for President*. New York: Stein and Day, 1977.

Stroud, Kandy. *How Jimmy Won*. New York: Morrow, 1977.

Wooten, James T. *Dasher: The Roots and the Rising of Jimmy Carter*. New York: Summit Books, 1978.

Part Three:
GERALD R. FORD

Ford, Betty. *The Times of My Life*. New York: Harper & Row, 1978.

Ford, Gerald R. *Public Papers of the Presidents of the U.S.*, containing the public messages, speeches, and statements of the President. Washington, D.C.: U.S. Government Printing Office, 1974–1978.

————. *The Speeches of President Gerald R. Ford, Presidential Campaign of 1976*. Washington, D.C.: U.S. Government Printing Office, 1977.

Hartmann, Robert T. *Palace Politics: An Inside Account of the Ford Years*. New York: McGraw-Hill, 1980.

Hersey, John. *The President*. New York: Knopf, 1975.

Kennerly, David Hume. *Shooter*. New York: Newsweek Books, 1979.

MacDougall, Malcolm. *We Almost Made It*. New York: Crown Publishers, 1977.

Mollenhoff, Clark. *The Man Who Pardoned Nixon.* New York: St. Martin's Press, 1976.

Reeves, Richard. *A Ford, Not a Lincoln.* New York: Harcourt Brace Jovanovich, 1975.

terHorst, Jerald. *Gerald Ford and the Future of the Presidency.* New York: J. Okpaku, 1975.

Vestal, Bud. *Jerry Ford, Up Close.* New York: Coward, McCann & Geoghegan, 1974.

Part Four:
RICHARD M. NIXON

Anson, Robert Sam. *Exile: The Unquiet Oblivion of Richard M. Nixon.* New York: Simon and Schuster, 1984.

Brodie, Farn McKay. *Richard Nixon: The Shaping of His Character.* New York: Norton, 1981.

Ehrlichman, John. *Witness to Power: The Nixon Years.* New York: Simon and Schuster, 1982.

Evans, Rowland. *Nixon in the White House.* New York: Random House, 1971.

Klein, Herbert. *Making It Perfectly Clear.* Garden City, N.Y.: Doubleday, 1980.

Lurie, Leonard. *The Running of Richard Nixon.* New York: Coward, McCann & Geoghegan, 1972.

Mazlish, Bruce. *In Search of Nixon: A Psychohistorical Inquiry.* New York: Basic Books, 1972.

McGinniss, Joe. *The Selling of the President.* New York: Trident Press, 1969.

Nixon, Richard M. *Public Papers of the Presidents of the U.S.,* containing the public messages, speeches, and statements of the President. Washington, D.C.: U.S. Government Printing Office, 1969–1974.

———. *The Speeches of President Richard M. Nixon, Presidential Campaign of 1972.* Washington, D.C.: U.S. Government Printing Office, 1973.

————. *The Speeches of Richard M. Nixon, Presidential Campaign of 1968.* Washington, D.C.: U.S. Government Printing Office, 1969.

————. *The Speeches of Vice President Richard M. Nixon, Presidential Campaign of 1960.* Washington, D.C.: U.S. Government Printing Office, 1961.

Osborne, John. *The Last Nixon Watch.* Washington, D.C.: New Republic, 1975.

————. *The Nixon Watch.* New York: Liveright, 1970.

————. *The Second Year of the Nixon Watch.* New York: Liveright, 1971.

————. *The Third Year of the Nixon Watch.* New York: Liverwright, 1971

Price, Raymond. *With Nixon.* New York: Viking Press, 1977.

Safire, William. *Before the Fall.* New York: Doubleday, 1975.

Vidal, Gore. *An Evening with Richard Nixon.* New York: Random House, 1972.

Part Five:
LYNDON B. JOHNSON

Adler, Bill, ed. *The Johnson Humor.* New York: Simon and Schuster, 1965.

Baker, Leonard. *The Johnson Eclipse: A President's Vice Presidency.* New York: Macmillan, 1966.

Bishop, Jim. *A Day in the Life of President Johnson.* New York: Random House, 1967.

Caro, Robert. *The Years of Lyndon Johnson.* New York: Knopf, 1982.

Carpenter, Liz. *Ruffles and Flourishes.* Garden City, N.Y.: Doubleday, 1970.

Christian, George. *The President Steps Down.* New York: Macmillan, 1970.

Cormier, Frank. *LBJ—The Way He Was.* Garden City, N.Y.: Doubleday, 1977.

Dugger, Ronnie, *The Politician: The Life and Times of Lyndon Johnson.* New York: Norton, 1982.

Evans, Rowland. *Lyndon B. Johnson: The Exercise of Power*. New York: New American Library, 1966.

Goldman, Eric. *The Tragedy of Lyndon Johnson*. New York: Knopf, 1969.

Johnson, Claudia Alta. *A White House Diary*. New York: Holt, Rinehart & Winson, 1970.

Johnson, Lyndon Baines. *Public Papers of the Presidents of the U.S.*, containing the public messages, speeches, and statements of the President. Washington, D.C.: U.S. Government Printing Office, 1963–1967.

————. *The Speeches of President Lyndon B. Johnson, Presidential Campaign of 1964*. Washington, D.C.: U.S. Government Printing Office, 1965.

Kearns, Doris. *Lyndon Johnson and the American Dream*. New York: Harper & Row, 1976.

Miller, Merle. *Lyndon: An Oral Biography*. New York: Putnam, 1980.

Reedy, George E. *Lyndon B. Johnson: A Memoir*. New York: Andrews and McMeel, 1982.

Sidey, Hugh. *A Very Personal Presidency*. New York: Atheneum, 1968.

Valenti, Jack. *A Very Human President*. New York: Norton, 1975.

White, William Smith. *The Professional: Lyndon B. Johnson*. Boston, Houghton Mifflin, 1964.

Wicker, Tom. *JFK and LBJ: The Influence of Personality Upon Politics*. New York: Morrow, 1968.

Part Six:
JOHN F. KENNEDY

Adler, Bill, ed. *The Complete Kennedy Wit*. New York: Gramarcy Publishing, 1967.

Bradlee, Benjamin. *Conversations with Kennedy*. New York: Norton, 1975.

Brayman, Harold. *The President Speaks off the Record*. New York: Dow Jones Books, 1976.

Burns, James MacGregor. *John Kennedy: A Political Profile*. New York: Harcourt Brace, 1960.

Collier, Peter, and Horowitz, David. *The Kennedys*. New York: Summit Books, 1984.

Fay. P. B. *The Pleasure of His Company*. New York: Harper & Row, 1966.

Gardner, Gerald, ed. *The Quotable Mr. Kennedy*. New York: Abelard Schuman, 1962.

———. *The Shining Moments*. New York: Pocket Books, 1963.

Gardner, John, ed. *To Turn the Tide*. New York: Harper & Row, 1962.

Kennedy, John F. *The Speeches of Senator John F. Kennedy, Presidential Campaign of 1960*. Washington, D.C.: U.S. Government Printing Office, 1961

Mailer, Norman. *The Presidential Papers*. New York: Putnam, 1963.

Manchester, William. *One Brief Shining Moment*. Boston: Little, Brown, 1983.

———. *Portrait of a President*. Boston: Little, Brown, 1962.

O'Donnell, Kenneth P., and Powers, David F. *Johnny, We Hardly Knew Ye*. Boston: Little, Brown, 1972.

Paper, Lewis J. *The Promise and the Performance: The Leadership of John F. Kennedy*. New York: Crown Publishers, 1975.

Salinger, Pierre. *With Kennedy*. Garden City, N.Y.: Doubleday, 1966.

Schlesinger, Arthur, Jr. *A Thousand Days: John F. Kennedy in the White House*. Boston: Houghton Mifflin, 1965.

Sidney, Hugh. *John F. Kennedy, President*. New York: Atheneum, 1964.

Smith, Merriman. *The Good New Days*. Indianapolis: Bobbs-Merrill, 1962.

Sorensen, Theodore C. *Kennedy*. New York: Harper & Row, 1965.

———. *The Kennedy Legacy*. New York: Macmillan, 1969.

Index